CIVIL DISOBEDIENCE

MANIFESTO

**WORDS
THAT
CHANGED
THE WORLD**

CIVIL DISOBEDIENCE

Andrew Kirk

BARRON'S

First edition for the United States, its territories and possessions,
and Canada published in 2004 by Barron's Educational Series, Inc.
by arrangement with the Ivy Press Limited

All inquiries should be addressed to:
Barron's Educational Series, Inc.,
250 Wireless Boulevard
Hauppauge, New York 11788
www.barronseduc.com

International Standard Book Number
0-7641-2866-3

Library of Congress Catalog Card No. 2003116941

This book was conceived,
designed, and produced by
THE IVY PRESS LIMITED
The Old Candlemakers
West Street, Lewes
East Sussex, BN7 2NZ, U.K.

Creative Director Peter Bridgewater
Publisher Sophie Collins
Editorial Director Jason Hook
Designer Jane Lanaway
Picture Researcher Vanessa Fletcher
Project Editor Caroline Earle

Printed in China
9 8 7 6 5 4 3 2 1

CIVIL DISOBEDIENCE

CIVIL
DISOBEDIENCE
INTRODUCTION

Henry David Thoreau's essay "Civil Disobedience" is probably the most famous short work in American literature. It has been published in dozens of editions and appears on curriculums for schools and colleges throughout America. It is one of those few works to have introduced a new expression into the English language, although ironically the term "civil disobedience" does not appear in Thoreau's essay or anywhere else in his writings. This book gives a brief introduction to the essay, setting it in its historical context and offering an account of how it came to enjoy its current reputation.

Henry Thoreau was born on July 12, 1817, in Concord, Massachusetts, and died in the same village 44 years later of tuberculosis, on May 6, 1862. After graduating from Harvard College he worked intermittently in his family's pencil-making business and as a schoolteacher, opening a private school with his brother John (he had resigned from his first job in a public school after only two weeks, having been reprimanded for not beating his pupils often enough). He later helped Ralph Waldo Emerson to edit the Transcendentalist magazine *The Dial*, and he finished his working life as a land surveyor, which gave him ample opportunity to make the observations of the flora and fauna that guaranteed his subsequent fame as a naturalist.

Thoreau wrote throughout his life, although he published only two books in his lifetime, *A Week on the Concord and Merrimack Rivers* and *Walden*. His works encompassed scientific botanical studies (a work on forest

A daguerreotype of Thoreau made in 1856 when he was 39 years old. This is one of only two known photographic images of the writer.

growth is still accepted by botanists today), travel writing, poetry, natural history, and his *Journal*, begun in 1837. Thoreau started the journal as a practice book for his more formal writings, but it soon became a literary work in itself and is central to his present literary status. He also wrote and lectured on social and political subjects, particularly slavery, and "Civil Disobedience," originally delivered as a lecture in 1848, is one of a series of essays written in support of the abolitionist cause.

Thoreau was little known in his own day outside the immediate circle of his friends and the other New England Transcendentalists. He had a reputation as a difficult and prickly personality, rather stern and unbending, and it has often been suggested that he was happiest in his own company. Although his books were read in Europe, for various reasons he remained an obscure figure in America well into the twentieth century. However, his rise to fame, once under way, was meteoric, and the aim of this book is to try to account for Thoreau's progress from cranky nineteenth-century naturalist to poster boy for the 1960s counterculture. One of the most intriguing aspects of Thoreau is the openness of his work to multiple, even contradictory, interpretations. The chapters that follow explore the many different versions of Thoreau that have emerged over the past century, finally considering the value of his writing and thinking in the context of the problems and the potential of the twenty-first century.

Thoreau's birthplace in Concord, Massachusetts. Except for a brief period when he was tutoring Emerson's brother's children in Staten Island, Thoreau lived in Concord all his adult life.

CIVIL
DISOBEDIENCE
CONTEXT
AND
CREATOR

In January 1848, when Henry David Thoreau stood up in the Lyceum in Concord, Massachusetts, to deliver his lecture on "The Rights and Duties of the Individual in Relation to Government" (later known as "Civil Disobedience"), the United States of America had been in existence for a little more than 70 years. Born out of the Revolutionary War of 1775–1783 and grounded in the originating documents drawn up by Jefferson, Adams, Washington, and the other founding fathers, America was unique in being an ideal state, a creation of the people for the people. Whereas the old European colonial powers had grown organically over centuries of invasion, settlement, and annexation, America was a modern invention, self-consciously established on republican lines that harked back to a classical age, with democracy as its bedrock. This was a new start in a new continent, with the hostile frontier waiting to be conquered and the American people and their own resources ready for the challenge.

However open to contradiction by the realities of the historical record this idealized account might be, and however tarnished by the subsequent actions of the settlers in conquering the West, it is nonetheless immensely important in a mythic sense—that is to say, as the story that U.S. citizens have made use of, and still make use of, in defining themselves and their relations with each other and with other nations. It is a story that helps to explain the tradition of writing to which Thoreau belongs, and the reasons he felt obliged to speak as he did in the Concord Lyceum.

The outbreak of hostilities at Lexington Common, near Concord, in April 1775 resulted in the first British defeat and heralded eight years of war.

The drawing up of the Declaration of Independence by Thomas Jefferson and his fellows was the beginning of a conscious process that led to the establishment of the world's first modern democracy.

The Foundation Documents

The Declaration of Independence, the U.S. Constitution, and the Bill of Rights are without doubt the best known and most quoted political documents ever written.

We hold these truths to be self-evident, that all men are created equal, that they are endowed by their Creator with certain unalienable Rights, that among these are Life, Liberty and the pursuit of Happiness.—That to secure these rights, Governments are instituted among Men, deriving their just powers from the consent of the governed.

The self-confidence of these words is not only breathtaking but also fitting for a brave new world. With regard to Thoreau, there are two important points to note here. The first is the idea of "happiness." What Jefferson and his fellows meant by this is open to debate. What they certainly did *not* mean was that America was to be a nation of hedonists, a permissive society with a moral obligation to have a nice day. The pursuit of happiness for political thinkers of Jefferson's time would have meant living the "good life," and this was a collective idea—that is, it related to the "common weal." Classical republicanism saw people as essentially political animals, and so all citizens were to have the right to participate in public affairs, to discuss, to deliberate, and to make decisions. Thoreau was intensely concerned with the idea of the "good life" and what that meant, and the importance of each individual's striving to discover for himself or herself what it meant. The Declaration of Independence placed

A statue of the hated George III is toppled in New York City during the Revolutionary War, in a painting by William Walcutt. The king's offenses against the American colonies formed the central passage of the Declaration of Independence.

considerable responsibility on the people themselves, and Thoreau took his responsibilities and those of his fellow Americans very seriously.

The second significant point for our purposes is the last part of this quotation: "governments are instituted among men, drawing their just powers from the consent of the governed." The American Revolution had been a reaction against unjust government—the rule of the English king, which the American colonists regarded as tyrannical, brutal, and illegitimate. Hence the Declaration of Independence and the Constitution after it were careful to set down what was permitted to government and what was not, and to establish a range of checks and balances in an effort to ensure that the exercise of power was not overweening, but was held within certain well-defined restraints. The relationship between the states and the federal government was thus defined, the ideal of free expression was supported with unprecedented guarantees, and the very idea of government was made contingent on the consent of those governed. In a sense, revolution and uncertainty were built into the system; the system was only in place for as long as it served its purpose, and if it ceased to do that, it could be dispensed with and a new system introduced. The idea that you might need to guarantee free speech was an admission that the truth might not always be a desirable commodity in the eyes of those who had the power.

The importance of this for Thoreau was that the system of government would work only if the individual was always alert to what was being done in his or her name, and willing and able to withhold consent if appropriate. If proper government relies on the consent of the people, then the people have to be sure that they know what the government is doing and, more important, that the government is doing what they as individuals think it should be doing. Thoreau's emphasis on the individual is paramount in "Civil Disobedience"; he is not concerned with the view of the majority. The primacy of the majority view is based on the assumption that the majority are physically the strongest, which as far as Thoreau is concerned is no justification for anything. For Thoreau, consent is a moral judgement for which each individual is accountable to his or her own conscience. This idea can be seen as relating directly to the fundamental documents that established the Union of which Thoreau was a citizen.

The habit of public meetings for citizens to address matters of common concern was part of the nineteenth-century American political culture.

Transcendentalism

The imperative of new ideas and new beginnings showed itself in areas other than politics. The Transcendentalist movement that emerged in New England in the 1830s had its roots in the Unitarian Church. Unitarianism was a reaction to the strict Calvinism of the first New England Puritans, whose central doctrines were the innate depravity of human beings through sin and the idea of the elect chosen by God's

THE UNITARIAN ARMS

Unitarianism developed in reaction against the spiritual aridity of the first settlers' Calvinism. The Unitarians wanted to find a place for ethics in the process of salvation, and aspects of Unitarian thought developed into Transcendentalism.

grace to be saved through the redemptive sacrifice of Christ. The emphasis was on the irreparable corruptness of human nature and the inscrutability of divine grace. Calvinism had no place for ethics and rendered a person's behavior and character irrelevant to his or her chances of salvation. The rigidity of these doctrines was a source of considerable debate among Puritan clergy, and over time many began to formulate more liberal views that made room for individual piety and ethical practice in the process of salvation. The culmination of these debates was the election of a theological liberal, Henry Ware, as Professor of Divinity at Harvard in 1805. This met with hostility from orthodox Calvinists, and led ultimately to the formation of the Unitarian Church in 1825, which had as the basis of its theological teaching the divine potential within each individual. In opposition to Calvinism, Unitarianism defined the spiritual life in terms of a continuing effort to cultivate one's own spiritual resources.

The founder of the Transcendentalist movement, and arguably of a genuinely American literary and philosophical culture, was himself a Unitarian minister, Ralph Waldo Emerson. His grandfather and his father were both Unitarian ministers, and after graduating from Harvard Divinity School, Emerson became the pastor of Boston's Second Unitarian Church in 1829. However, he resigned his pastorate in 1832, partly prompted by the untimely death of his first wife, partly as a semiconscious rebellion against his family heritage, but more fundamentally because of his dissatisfaction with

the narrowness of the vision of historical Christianity. Emerson wanted to escape the constraints of his religious background, and he effectively became a secular priest for a new vision, which came to be called Transcendentalism.

The first text of Transcendentalism was Emerson's book *Nature*, published in 1836. The opening page sets the tone for what was to be Emerson's lifetime enterprise:

> *Our age is retrospective. It builds the sepulchres of the fathers . . . the foregoing generations beheld God and nature face to face; we through their eyes . . . . Why should not we have a poetry and philosophy of insight and not of tradition, and a religion by revelation to us, and not the history of theirs?*

The basis of Emerson's vision in *Nature* was the idea of the "divinity in man," the power of the individual self to achieve spiritual nobility and grandeur, to rise above the mundane and the material and live in accordance with the higher law as divined through an intense contemplation of nature. The Transcendentalist movement was greatly influenced by the Romantic school in literature, particularly the work of Wordsworth, Coleridge, and Goethe, with the figure of the poet rather than the priest as, in Shelley's words, "the unacknowledged legislator of the world." But what Emerson strove to do was to create a specifically American culture from these Old World influences, to redeem America both from its cultural subservience to the established European civilization and from what he saw as its own incipient slide toward a degraded materialism.

Ralph Waldo Emerson is regarded by many as the father of a distinctively American culture, and his book *Nature* was the urtext of Transcendentalism.

Emerson's house in Concord. The presence of Emerson attracted a number of writers to the village, including Nathaniel Hawthorne, Margaret Fuller, and Bronson Alcott, such that it became an important intellectual and literary center in Thoreau's time.

In 1837 Emerson gave the graduation address at Harvard, later published as "The American Scholar." In the audience was Henry David Thoreau. It is not certain when Thoreau and Emerson met, although Emerson had moved to Thoreau's home village of Concord in 1834. What is certain is that Emerson was immensely influential for Thoreau. Thoreau had read *Nature*, being sufficiently impressed to give it to a friend as a graduation present, and Emerson had written to the president of Harvard in pursuit of a scholarship on his behalf. This gesture was characteristic of Emerson's pervasive presence throughout Thoreau's career as his guiding light, patron, friend, and ultimately his severest critic.

"The American Scholar" contains many ideas that were central to Thoreau's conception of the "good life" and his own later writings. Emerson sets out the role of the scholar in the present age, an age of revolution:

> *If there is any period one would desire to be born in, is it not the age of Revolution; when the old and the new stand side by side and admit of being compared . . . when the historic glories of the old can be compensated by the rich possibilities of the new era?*

He describes the sources of the scholar's education—books, experience, and most important, nature:

> *The first in time and the first in importance of the influences upon the mind is that of nature.*

Emerson views nature, as Wordsworth had done and as Thoreau would do, as the reflection of the human soul. For Emerson, nature was the supreme determining force in human lives. Thoreau was to make the study of nature the central theme of his work, although paradoxically this became one of the chief causes of the later estrangement between the two.

Emerson emphasizes the centrality of the individual to his vision:

Everything that tends to insulate the individual—to surround him with barriers of natural respect, so that each man shall feel the world is his, and man shall treat with man as a sovereign state with a sovereign state—tends to true union as well as greatness.

This also can be seen as a fundamental to Thoreau's philosophy, and time and again in "Civil Disobedience" he champions the importance and power of the individual against the masses, the herd mentality, and the state. Emerson finishes his talk with a clarion call to his listeners to redeem the culture of America:

Public and private avarice make the air that we breathe thick and fat . . . . The mind of this country, taught to aim at low objects, feeds upon itself . . . . We will walk on our own feet; we will work with our own hands; we will speak our own minds.

These ideas all chimed in with the tenor of Thoreau's own genius. Little wonder that Thoreau swiftly became one of Emerson's closest disciples.

The ideas of the English Romantics, such as William Wordsworth, were influential in shaping Emerson's philosophy, although Emerson was not impressed by Wordsworth himself when he met him in 1833.

Emerson's patronage was immensely important to the establishment of Thoreau's writing career, even to the extent of allowing the younger man to build the hut on his land near Walden Pond for the experiment in living that would become Thoreau's best-known book.

Thoreau and Emerson

The relationship between Thoreau and Emerson was complex, and it is impossible to examine it properly here. Emerson acted as Thoreau's patron in the early years of their association, advising him over the publication of his first book and employing him to assist with the editing of the Transcendentalist magazine *The Dial*. Thoreau stayed in Emerson's house, acted as tutor to his brother's children, and lived in a hut on his land by Walden Pond, the experience that later helped him produce his most famous book, *Walden*. In return, Emerson's own ideas were sparked by the vigor and originality of Thoreau's mind, and the promise of the fulfillment of his vision of a cultural enlightenment.

The relationship was undoubtedly imbalanced: Emerson was senior by 14 years and habitually referred in his journals to "my Henry," as if Thoreau were his own creation. Emerson had an independent income from his dead wife's estate to support his literary career, he was well connected in Boston by virtue of his family ties, and he was the acknowledged leader of the Transcendentalists. Thoreau, recently graduated, had few such advantages; he worked as a schoolteacher and in his family's pencil-making business. Each was in his own way a difficult personality. Emerson was, by his own admission, emotionally cold and reserved and uncomfortable in society. Thoreau for his part was prickly and somewhat intolerant of other people's weaknesses. However, the most intense period of their friendship constituted a meeting of two souls in an essential, almost mystical relation.

The demands of this rarefied type of relationship made it perhaps inevitable that it would collapse under the strain. A fundamental incompatibility existed between Transcendentalist devotion to the divinity of the self and the emotional tolerance and flexibility required to take account of human frailties in maintaining social relationships. The relationship between Emerson and Thoreau was characterized in their journals in terms of faith, trust, and nobleness. It was a connection in which the actuality of character and emotion and mundane circumstance did not register. Over time, however, Thoreau showed a disinclination to follow in the intellectual path that Emerson appeared to be establishing for him. When their philosophies began to diverge and their idealization of each other evaporated, "ordinary" friendship became extremely difficult because so much had been invested in the "ideal."

This estrangement is important for our purposes because it bore heavily on the way in which Thoreau's later reputation developed. By about 1849 the rift between Thoreau and Emerson was complete, and each was writing of the other with a mixture of disappointment, anger, and resignation. Emerson was appalled by what he regarded as his protegé's wasting of his talents in fruitless nature studies and eccentric reclusive experiments. He was frustrated by Thoreau's apparent lack of active engagement with society. Thoreau for his part was unhappy with Emerson's increasing adoption of what he regarded as the stultifying conformities of civilization:

The Thoreau pencil-making company was established in 1823, and Thoreau's periodic employment in his father's firm supplied a modest income.

When I consider what my friend's relations & acquaintances are—what his tastes & habits—then the difference between us gets named. I see that all these friends & acquaintances & tastes & habits are indeed my friend's self.

Emerson had been plunged into a spiritual crisis during the 1840s by the death of his infant son, but also by the failure of his literary "sons," Thoreau chief among them, to take up the challenge that had been offered in "The American Scholar:"

We see young men who owe us a new world, so readily and lavishly they promise but they never acquit the debt; they die young and dodge the account; or if they live, they lose themselves in the crowd.

Thoreau, painted in 1854 by Samuel Worcester Rowse. By this date Thoreau had struck out firmly on his own intellectual path independently of Emerson.

As Emerson's idealism seemed to be waning, to be replaced by an acceptance of limiting realities ("We live amid surfaces, and the true art of life is to skate upon them"), Thoreau was pursuing a radical individualism that refused to bend to the demands of the social and the civilized. Emerson made efforts to patch up the quarrel during the 1850s, but their fundamental philosophical differences remained insurmountable. Thoreau was repelled, for instance, by his friend's apparent enthusiasm for the material and social advancement he had found in Europe during his second visit in 1847. Their personal dispute dramatized the struggle for the heart of an American culture. However, Thoreau's early death in 1862 at the age of 44 left Emerson to have the last word—with an outcome that we examine in Chapter 3.

The Sources of Thoreau's Political Thought

The public lecture was a common mode of popular instruction in mid-nineteenth-century America, and almost every population center had its lecture hall, or lyceum. In 1839 there were 137 lyceums in Massachusetts alone, with established circuits giving a weekly platform to educational, scientific, literary, or political speakers. Emerson's main income came from his lecture tours, and lectures were a popular source of entertainment and education for the dark winter evenings. By the 1840s, slavery and abolitionism were regular platform subjects.

Thoreau's political ideas as expressed in "Civil Disobedience" were not especially original. Arguments regarding the proper relation of the individual to the state, the conflicting demands of private conscience and the law of the land, the idea of a social contract in which some personal freedoms are relinquished in return for the promise of a well-ordered society—all of these notions were current at the time Thoreau was writing and feature to some degree in his essay. What was unique to Thoreau was the force of his rhetoric and the symbolic power of his own experience. Perhaps unsurprisingly, an important forerunner of his work was an essay by Emerson, "Politics," published in 1844.

Emerson was temperamentally more conservative than Thoreau, and one feature of their later estrangement was Emerson's dismay at his young follower's prickly radicalism and antisociability. Indeed, "Politics" begins in a vein of apparent high Toryism, equating the higher law with

The public lecture circuit was so popular that Emerson could make a comfortable living, earning around $2,000 for a winter series of talks—four times the annual salary of a skilled worker.

By the time he was in his seventies, Emerson had become the elder statesman of American letters, and his writings had attracted, inspired, or provoked an array of American philosophers, poets, and novelists.

the power of property. Later in life, Emerson seemed to become pragmatically resigned to laissez-faire competition as the only basis for society: There might be casualties along the way, but the end result would be the best arrangement of society because it was most in tune with our fundamental nature. In 1844, however, Emerson retained a belief in the power of the individual, and most of his essay reflects on the shabbiness of government in comparison to the higher law, and the desirability of establishing a society on the basis of love rather than force. So there are passages in "Politics" that hint at Thoreau's position:

> The antidote to this abuse of formal government is the influence of private character, the growth of the Individual . . . the appearance of the wise man; of whom the existing government is, it must be owned, but a shabby imitation . . . . To educate the wise man the State exists, and with the appearance of the wise man the State expires.

This is one of the chief themes of Thoreau's essay: the importance of the wise man. It could be said that Thoreau's aim was to dramatize the power of the individual:

> There will never be a really free and enlightened State until the State comes to recognize the individual as a higher and independent power, from which all its own power and authority are derived, and treats him accordingly.

Toward the end of Emerson's essay we find the following passage:

There never was in any man sufficient faith in the
power of rectitude to inspire him with the broad
design of renovating the State on the principle
of right and love . . . . I do not call to mind a single
human being who has steadily denied the authority
of the laws, on the simple ground of his own
moral nature.

Maybe Thoreau saw this as a challenge of sorts. At any
event, it is not a large step to see the text that Thoreau
created from his action in denying the authority of the law by
withholding his poll tax as just this kind of broad design.

Emerson was characteristically ambivalent about
Thoreau's antigovernment action and imprisonment. In his
1846 journal he complained that "no government short of
a monarchy consisting of one king & one subject, will
appease you," and in conversation he reportedly referred to
Thoreau's action as "mean and skulking." He seemed to be
objecting to a strain of fanaticism in Thoreau—the same
kind of perverse contrariness that he described in his
later address at Thoreau's funeral. He accuses Thoreau of
wanting to escape from this "double faced equivocating
mixed Jesuitical universe." Of course, in a sense he is right;
Thoreau is stepping outside to speak as a prophet,
whereas Emerson would always hedge about, enquiring into
motives and consequences and apparently holding back
from action. There is a well-known story that Emerson
visited Thoreau in jail and asked in exasperation, "Why are
you here?" Thoreau's acerbic response was "Why are you

Right: **The Fugitive Slave Law** required the Northern states to return escaped slaves to their owners, and was vehemently opposed by many New Englanders, including Emerson.

Far right: ***Aesthetic Papers***, in which "Civil Disobedience" was first published under the title "Resistance to Civil Government." The journal was intended by its editor, Elizabeth Peabody, to be an idealistic forum for a wide range of views. However, the first issue proved to be the last, attracting only fifty subscribers.

not here?" The story is almost certainly apocryphal, and after the slave-power-appeasing Missouri Compromise of 1850, Emerson did come to the aid of the party and was one of the first and most vocal opponents of the newly reenacted Fugitive Slave Law. There was nonetheless a degree of unwillingness on Emerson's part to act on the logic of his arguments that was not shared by Thoreau.

By 1849 when Thoreau's lecture was published in *Aesthetic Papers*, Emerson's position seemed to have altered. He published an essay, "War," written in 1838, in the same journal, and must have expected it to be read as reinforcing Thoreau's lecture:

> *a man must be responsible, with goods, health and life, for his behavior; . . . should be himself a kingdom and a state; . . . quite willing to use the opportunities and advantages that good government throws in his way, but nothing daunted, and not really the poorer if government, law and order went by the board . . . .*

Thoreau says much the same thing, but goes on to show how the state opposes such self-reliance:

For my own part, I should not like to think that I ever rely on the protection of the State. But, if I deny the authority of the State when it presents its tax-bill, it will soon take and waste all my property, and so harass me and my children without end. This is hard. This makes it impossible for a man to live honestly, and at the same time comfortably in outward respects.

The only resort then, says Thoreau, is to become a kingdom to yourself:

You must hire or squat somewhere, and raise but a small crop, and eat that soon. You must live within yourself, and depend upon yourself always tucked up and ready for a start, and not have many affairs.

Emerson was to object to Thoreau's apparent withdrawal from the world, but what Thoreau is trying to find is a way to live deliberately with principle. He is not looking for a fight, as Emerson seemed to suggest:

I came into the world, not chiefly to make this a good place to live in, but to live in it, be it good or bad.

The absolute necessity of living according to the higher law, the divinity in man, the truth of one's spirit—call it what you will—is the basis of Thoreau's politics, and his resistance to the state comes at those points where this way of living is rendered impossible.

Thoreau's withdrawal to his hut by Walden pond was intended not as a renunciation of the world but as an experiment to show how simply one might live.

Thomas Carlyle and William Paley

Two other writers were influential on Thoreau's politics—one as an inspiration, the other as an opponent. Thomas Carlyle was the son of Scottish Presbyterians and had originally trained for the ministry. Although he abandoned his Puritan faith, he retained a puritanical outlook of passionate idealism and devotion to the idea of the spirit as a higher truth in revolt against materialist, mechanistic, "civilized" society. The two men admired each other's writings, and Carlyle was the only writer to be made the subject of a comprehensive study by Thoreau. From Carlyle, Thoreau took two important themes. One was the primacy of inner conviction over outward conformity. "Law never made men a whit more just," says Thoreau in his essay: What matters is justice and what is right, regardless of whether that concurs with what your neighbors think, the law of the land, or the Constitution itself.

Thomas Carlyle, whose enthusiasm for the heroic in his writings struck a chord with Thoreau.

Thoreau also shared Carlyle's admiration for the hero, the righteous individual who acts as a beacon for society. In Carlyle's view the conflicts and problems of modern society would be resolved by the wisdom of the few rather than the organization of the many, and in *On Heroes, Hero Worship and the Heroic in History* Carlyle exemplified this idea with studies of great men from the fields of literature, religion, and politics. Thoreau's essay is similarly a paean to the power of the righteous individual against the force of the unthinking majority: "Any man more right than his neighbors constitutes a majority of one already."

Thoreau's oppositional influence was William Paley, the Archdeacon of Carlisle (in northern England) and author of *Principles of Moral and Political Philosophy.* Paley's theological utilitarianism equated ethical behavior with a prudent desire for heavenly reward. The only basis for good behavior was self-interest: "Christ came into the world to tell us that we should all go to hell if our actions did not tend to promote the greatest happiness of the greatest numbers" was how one commentator summarized Paley's position. Paley's politics derived from this ethical viewpoint. As long as the government upholds the interest of general society, it should be obeyed; revolution and resistance are to be avoided because they tend to produce unforeseen and unwanted side effects. Expediency, in Paley's view, was the only consideration with regard to questions of government.

The utilitarianism of William Paley was the antithesis of Thoreau's commitment to righteous, rather than prudential, action.

Thoreau viewed this standpoint with contempt, and because Paley has a chapter on the "Duty of Submission to Civil Government," so Thoreau makes his intentions clear in calling his essay "Resistance to Civil Government" (later entitled "Civil Disobedience," *see page 35*). Expediency simply means the government of the strongest—those with the greatest force or the greatest numbers on their side. Thoreau is concerned with the inalienability of the individual conscience. The greatest good of the greatest number is a morally vacuous idea for him, as is the notion that the preservation of civil society should be the only aim of government. Prudential considerations were important at the level of means, but no further. The end of

For President Abraham Lincoln, the Civil War was not a struggle to abolish slavery, but the inevitable response to the Southern states' secession from the Union which it was his duty to preserve.

government had to be judged on moral grounds, and the majority was not a moral entity:

> *If I have unjustly wrested a plank from a drowning man, I must restore it to him though I drown myself. This, according to Paley, would be inconvenient. But he that would save his life, in such a case, shall lose it. This people must cease to hold slaves, and to make war on Mexico, though it cost them their existence as a people.*

Thoreau always judges political action at the bar of morality. And he was sufficiently clear-sighted about the consequences of his position to recognize the possibility of civil war a dozen years before it broke out. We can compare his statements with that of one of the greatest politicians of the day, Abraham Lincoln. Lincoln wrote to the newspaper editor Horace Greeley in 1862:

> *My paramount object in this struggle* is *to save the Union and is* not *either to save or to destroy slavery. If I could save the Union without freeing* any *slave I would do it; if I could save it by freeing* all *the slaves I would do it; and if I could save it by freeing some and leaving others alone, I would also do that.*

Lincoln's words reflect the pragmatism of the politician; Thoreau's, the idealism of the prophet. But by the time the Civil War broke out, Thoreau was fatally ill with tuberculosis. His initial support for the Northern cause seemed to wane as his health declined, and his apparently dismissive opinion of the great struggle was to be held against him after his death.

The Immediate Context of "Civil Disobedience"

The mainspring of Thoreau's lecture was his profound opposition to slavery and to the Mexican War of 1846, which was widely regarded in the North as a proslavery war. Slavery had been a foundation of the American colonies since their establishment, and although it would not be true to say that the United States could never have been created without slavery, the use of this cheap and captive labor source certainly enhanced the profitability of the tobacco, rice, and indigo plantations. By the mid-nineteenth century, slavery had ceased to be economically important in the North, but it remained an institution in the Southern states, where cotton was the main cash crop and the chief source of wealth. Equally significant was the social and cultural meaning of the practice. The ownership of land and of the slaves who worked the land established the status of the Southern elite; the abolition of slavery would mean, in Southern eyes, the dismemberment of the civilized culture of the Southern gentleman and the destruction of the social hierarchy in which everyone knew his or her place.

This idealized picture of the plantation system reflects the paternalistic view offered by the Southern elite of a slave population that was content with its lot and unwilling to have self-determination thrust upon it.

By the 1830s slavery was coming to be seen as increasingly at odds with the spirit of the times. The evangelical revival that was sweeping America led to a commitment to good works of every kind and a driving out of sin—and slavery was considered the chief of sins. At the same time, the rational philosophy of the Enlightenment portrayed slavery as fundamentally degrading to both the slaves and the slaveowners and as having no place in a modern society. The abolition of slavery in Britain's West Indian colonies in 1833 also gave impetus to the abolitionists in America.

The intransigence of the South in defending the institution was exacerbated by the radicalism of the main abolitionist voices in the North. Chief among these was William Lloyd Garrison, whose newspaper *The Liberator*, established in Boston in 1831, was the mouthpiece for the most strongly held abolitionist views. Garrison was an anarchist, and apart from his hostility to slavery his views on a number of other issues—for example, his proto-feminist criticism of the position of women in society and his attacks on the Sabbath and Christian ministry—were far in advance of what mainstream society found acceptable. Although it had only a small readership, the flamboyant style of *The Liberator* meant that its articles portraying a barbaric

William Lloyd Garrison and his newspaper *The Liberator* were instrumental in polarizing the views of North and South over the slave issue.

and brutish Southern aristocracy were widely reprinted, and it was assumed in the South to be representative of a much greater depth of antislavery feeling in the North than was the case. This fostered a sense of besieged paranoia, which produced in its turn extremist responses to perceived Northern threats to Southern culture. In fact, abolitionist feeling was not widespread in the North, and even among abolitionists Garrison was viewed as a dangerous revolutionary fanatic.

Northern opposition to slavery was rooted not so much in sympathy for the plight of the enslaved negroes as in fear of the security risk posed by large numbers of disaffected aliens. Large slave insurrections were relatively rare (not surprisingly, in light of the ferocity with which they were put down), but there was a significant rebellion in Virginia in 1831 that was more than enough to feed both Northern and Southern anxieties on the issue. Added to this was the sense that the agricultural economy of the South had had its day, and that the future lay in commerce and industry, the keystones of the Northern economy. The Northern states were determined, therefore, that as the westward expansion of the United States continued, newly claimed land on the frontier should be free rather than being co-opted by the slave economy. The "slaveocracy," of course, wanted more land put under cultivation, which meant more slaves. The issue was one of power politics rather than

The slave rebellion led by Nat Turner in 1831 resulted in the deaths of 55 white people and produced a frenzied reaction, with more than 200 slaves being killed by white mobs in addition to those executed by the state.

Antonio López de Santa Anna (above right) and President James K. Polk (above), opponents in the Mexican War of 1846–1848. The U.S. victory led to the annexation of the territory that became California and New Mexico.

antislavery sentiment, but as each side became more extravagant in its claims and counteraccusations, anti-Southern hostility in the North increased, and slavery was its focus. By the time Thoreau came to write his essay in 1848, the issue had become a source of bitter conflict between the Northern and Southern states of the Union.

The Mexican War was related to this conflict about the strength of the slaveowning faction in the Union. Texas, along with Mexico and California, had constituted a Spanish colony since the early sixteenth century. Moves for independence from the colonial power had begun in the early nineteenth century, and were focused in Texas as the area farthest geographically from the colonial capital, Mexico City. A series of insurrections with varying degrees of success ended in the establishment of Mexican independence in 1821, but the status of Texas had become uncertain over the course of the independence struggle.

America had made claims to Texas while it was still under Spanish control, but these were renounced under a treaty of 1819. Nonetheless, many Americans settled in Texas after Mexican independence, with the encouragement of the Mexican government. Power in Mexico was disputed between the Centralists, who favored dictatorial government, and the Federalists, who were republican democrats. By 1834, Antonio López de Santa Anna had managed to install himself as dictator. Federalist opposition to the dictatorship had its stronghold in Texas, and what became known as the

This banner for Polk's campaign, with the extra star representing Texas, reflects the explicit expansionist platform on which the president was elected.

Texas Revolution began in 1835. By the end of hostilities in April 1836, what had begun as a civil war of opposition to the Mexican government had turned into a war of independence as Texas was declared a republic.

Texas was recognized by the United States in 1837, and the Republic began to petition for admission to the Union. This was strongly opposed by the Northern abolitionists, because Texas, as a slave state, would increase the influence of the proslavery South. Congress became enmeshed in a long period of petitions and counterpetitions. However, the deadlock was broken by the presidential election of 1844, which was won by the Democrat James Polk on the basis of an expansionist policy calling for the annexation of lands to the southwest and west of the Union, including the state of Texas.

Texas was duly offered, and accepted, admission to the Union in 1845, and the United States placed an army of occupation in Texas to defend it against any Mexican attack. Nationalist sentiment in Mexico, which had never accepted the independence of Texas, was inflamed by this, and war with the United States became inevitable. The North was thus drawn into an armed conflict on behalf of the slaveholding power in the South, in the name of the United States.

Wendell Phillips was a lawyer and an important member of the Anti-Slavery Society of which Garrison was the president. Phillips was the most accomplished orator in the abolitionist camp, and after slavery was abolished he went on to campaign for women's rights and universal suffrage.

Thoreau's Protest

The only legal method of resolving the issue of slavery was a constitutional amendment: The Constitution permitted to each state in the Union the right to determine its own affairs, and an amendment required the ratification of three-quarters of the member states. However, in 1848, 15 of the 30 states were slave states, and there was no chance of any such amendment being passed. The Founding Fathers had thus bequeathed an intractable problem to their successors. Wendell Phillips, the most articulate abolitionist campaigner of his day, referred to the Constitution as a "proslavery compact." In light of the polarization of opinion between North and South on the issue of slavery, the political system held little hope for altering the situation. As far as Thoreau was concerned, electoral politics was pointless anyway—he refers to it as "a form of gaming"—and he did not bother to vote, not wanting it to be assumed that he concurred with the political process. In his essay, Thoreau faintly praises Massachusetts Senator Daniel Webster as a good politician, but points out that his political excellence lies in his qualities of prudence and expediency, both derogatory terms in the Thoreauvian moral lexicon.

With no apparent political or legal route open, Thoreau chose to step outside the institutional framework of society and opposed slavery on the strongest ground possible—that of morality, appealing to the conscience of each individual. He urges each person to "Cast your whole vote, not a strip of paper merely, but your whole influence," meaning that individuals should not simply rely on politicians but take an active part in affairs. He suggests that jail is the only place for an honest man in a slave state and refuses to recognize a "political organization as [his] government which is the *slave's* government also." Massachusetts was the Northern state most strongly opposed to slavery, and a significant center for abolitionist agitation. Thoreau thus had a basis of sympathy that he hoped to radicalize with his lecture.

The kernel of Thoreau's lecture is his account of the night he spent in jail for nonpayment of his poll tax. Thoreau had not paid the state poll tax since 1843, probably as a protest against the complicity of Massachusetts in returning fugitive slaves to their owners. The federal Fugitive Slave Act of 1793 required the nonslavery states not to harbor escapees from the South. In 1842 an attempt to return a black man named George Latimer to slavery had created a storm of protest in the state, and the strength of feeling was such that a state law was passed in 1843 forbidding any officer of the state from assisting in the return of fugitive slaves.

Senator Daniel Webster of Massachusetts attracted widespread contempt among abolitionists for his advocacy of the Fugitive Slave Law in the Senate in 1850 as part of the Missouri Compromise, aimed at preserving the Union and defusing the slavery crisis.

Why three years elapsed between Thoreau's ceasing to pay his poll tax and his being imprisoned is not clear. Nonpayment of the poll tax was not unusual, but the reason was more often poverty than ideology. People who did not pay were not allowed to vote, but the authorities

Bronson Alcott was a member of the Transcendentalist circle in Concord and an abolitionist campaigner. During the riots that followed the arrest of a fugitive slave, Anthony Burns, in Boston in 1854, Alcott famously formed a one-man deputation to the Boston courthouse to demand his release.

seldom pursued them because they generally had no property to seize in respect of the debt. Bronson Alcott and Charles Lane, two abolitionists, also refused to pay the poll tax as a protest against slavery in 1843, and they were arrested but released when the tax was paid on their behalf. Thoreau stopped paying soon afterward, but he was not apprehended. This may have been because his was an individual act of protest: Lane and Alcott belonged to the Garrisonian abolitionist organization, and were therefore more vocal and more visible. It may also have been because the Concord tax-collector, Sam Staples, was a hunting companion of Thoreau.

At the beginning of the Mexican War in 1846, however, Thoreau may have felt the need to make his protest more public. He wrote an article in the *Boston Courier*, protesting the war and expounding the principle of the centrality of the individual conscience: "If the national law bids me do what my conscience forbids, must not my conscience be supreme?" Thoreau stated that he would refuse to serve in the U.S. army in the war against Mexico. Because there was no conscription to the Mexican War, this was not an actual issue, but it was a means by which Thoreau could introduce the idea of civil disobedience as a way of expressing moral opposition.

A month after the publication of this article he met Sam Staples by chance, and they discussed his nonpayment. Staples suggested negotiating a reduced payment or lending Thoreau the money to pay, but Thoreau

The Concord tax-collector Sam Staples, who put Thoreau in jail and refused to go back to release him after the debt was paid because, according to his daughter's account, he had already taken his boots off and settled down for the evening.

refused. He may have decided to force the issue as a way of making his protest more concrete. In any event, Staples said that if Thoreau didn't pay he would have to go to jail, and Thoreau said that now was as good a time as any—and so Thoreau spent his night in Concord's jailhouse. In fact his aunt paid his debt soon after his arrival in the jail, much to Thoreau's annoyance, although he was not released until the following day, perhaps because of Staples's irritation with his friend's apparent pig-headedness. So the event on which the essay hinges was in itself relatively trivial, but Thoreau, through the force of his rhetoric, was able to imbue it with enormous symbolic power: "It matters not how small the beginning may seem to be: what is once well done is done forever."

As is common with many prophets, Thoreau's essay has been interpreted in different ways by both its admirers and its detractors. For one thing, the expression "civil disobedience" is never actually used in the essay, and the original title when the work was published was "Resistance to Civil Government." The title "Civil Disobedience" that we know today was adopted when the essay was republished in a posthumous collection of Thoreau's shorter works in 1866, perhaps because his editors were sensitive to allusions to the recent Confederate rebellion and Civil War. The change of title dilutes the assertiveness of the essay: "Disobedience" suggests that the institution being disobeyed has some kind of legitimacy and is permitted to respond with punishment,

John Brown was the apotheosis of the Transcendentalist hero for Thoreau, a man who acted according to his inner light without thought for the consequences. Thoreau describes Brown as a Christlike figure who sacrificed himself "to be the savior of four millions of men."

whereas "resistance" has more of the idea of a force being met by an opposing force. Thoreau does not in fact admit in the essay that a protestor is obliged to accept legal punishment.

Nor does Thoreau rule out the use of violence in pursuit of justice, contrary to popular belief: "But even suppose blood should flow. Is there not a sort of blood shed when the conscience is wounded?" A later essay was written in defense of John Brown, the abolitionist who was hanged for leading a violent attack on the U.S. Armory at Harper's Ferry, Virginia, with the intention of launching a slave insurrection. Thoreau's view of John Brown as a hero is at odds with the image that he later acquired as an advocate of nonviolent resistance. Thoreau's contemporary reputation as an "inflammatory" writer is evidenced by his inclusion in a list of Northern abolitionists by a Southern writer, Mary Boykin Chesnut, who wrote in her *Diary from Dixie*:

> *[they] live in nice New England homes, clean,*
> *sweet-smelling, shut up in libraries, writing books*
> *which ease their hearts of their bitterness against*
> *us. What self-denial do they practice to tell John*
> *Brown to come down here and cut our throats*
> *in Christ's name?*

There are thus a number of misconceptions about Thoreau and his essay. In a sense this does not matter except from the point of view of academic accuracy. Thoreau's intention was to arouse his audience's conscience, and the evidence of the twentieth century testifies to his success in this. Chapter 4 of this book sheds more light on the uses to which Thoreau's work was put—and the persona that came to be associated with him.

I heartily accept the motto,—"That government is best which governs least"; and I should like to see it acted up to more rapidly and systematically. Carried out, it finally amounts to this, which also I believe,— "That government is best which governs not at all"; and when men are prepared for it, that will be the kind of government which they will have. Government is at best but an expedient; but most governments are usually, and all governments are sometimes, inexpedient. The objections which have been brought against a standing army, and they are many and weighty, and deserve to prevail, may also at last be brought against a standing government. The standing army is only an arm of the standing government. The government itself, which is only the mode which the people have chosen to execute their will, is equally liable to be abused and perverted before the people can act through it. Witness the present Mexican war, the work of comparatively a few individuals using the standing government as their tool; for, in the outset, the people would not have consented to this measure.

This American government,—what is it but a tradition, though a recent one, endeavoring to transmit itself unimpaired to posterity, but each instant losing some of its integrity? It has not the vitality and force of a single living man; for a single man can bend it to his will. It is a sort of wooden gun to the people themselves. But it is not the less

necessary for this; for the people must have some
complicated machinery or other, and hear its din,
to satisfy that idea of government which they have.
Governments show thus how successfully men can
be imposed on, even impose on themselves, for their
own advantage. It is excellent, we must all allow.
Yet this government never of itself furthered any
enterprise, but by the alacrity with which it got out
of its way. It does not keep the country free. It does
not settle the West. It does not educate. The character
inherent in the American people has done all that
has been accomplished; and it would have done
somewhat more, if the government had not
sometimes got in its way. For government is an
expedient by which men would fain succeed in letting
one another alone; and, as has been said, when it is
most expedient, the governed are most let alone by it.
Trade and commerce, if they were not made of India-
rubber, would never manage to bounce over the
obstacles which legislators are continually putting in
their way; and, if one were to judge these men wholly
by the effects of their actions, and not partly by their
intentions, they would deserve to be classed and
punished with those mischievous persons who put
obstructions on the railroads.

But, to speak practically and as a citizen, unlike
those who call themselves no-government men, I ask
for, not at once no government, but at once a better

government. Let every man make known what kind of government would command his respect, and that will be one step toward obtaining it.

After all, the practical reason why, when the power is once in the hands of the people, a majority are permitted, and for a long period continue, to rule is not because they are most likely to be in the right, nor because this seems fairest to the minority, but because they are physically the strongest. But a government in which the majority rule in all cases cannot be based on justice, even as far as men understand it. Can there not be a government in which majorities do not virtually decide right and wrong, but conscience?—in which majorities decide only those questions to which the rule of expediency is applicable? Must the citizen ever for a moment, or in the least degree, resign his conscience to the legislator? Why has every man a conscience, then? I think that we should be men first, and subjects afterward. It is not desirable to cultivate a respect for the law, so much as for the right. The only obligation which I have a right to assume is to do at any time what I think right. It is truly enough said that a corporation has no conscience; but a corporation of conscientious men is a corporation with a conscience. Law never made men a whit more just; and, by means of their respect for it, even the well-disposed are daily made the agents of injustice.

*A common and natural result of an undue respect for
law is, that you may see a file of soldiers, colonel,
captain, corporal, privates, powder-monkeys, and all,
marching in admirable order over hill and dale to the
wars, against their wills, ay, against their common
sense and consciences, which makes it very steep
marching indeed, and produces a palpitation of the
heart. They have no doubt that it is a damnable
business in which they are concerned; they are all
peaceably inclined. Now, what are they? Men at all?
or small movable forts and magazines, at the service
of some unscrupulous man in power? . . .*

Thoreau compares the service that the mass of men give
the state as that of soldiers in the army, "as machines,
with their bodies."

*How does it become a man to behave toward this
American government to-day? I answer, that he
cannot without disgrace be associated with it.
I cannot for an instant recognize that political
organization as my government which is the* slave's
government *also.*

*All men recognize the right of revolution; that is,
the right to refuse allegiance to, and to resist, the
government, when its tyranny or its inefficiency are
great and unendurable. But almost all say that such
is not the case now. But such was the case, they
think, in the Revolution of '75. If one were to tell me
that this was a bad government because it taxed*

certain foreign commodities brought to its ports, it is
most probable that I should not make an ado about
it, for I can do without them. All machines have their
friction; and possibly this does enough good to
counterbalance the evil. At any rate, it is a great evil
to make a stir about it. But when the friction comes
to have its machine, and oppression and robbery are
organized, I say, let us not have such a machine any
longer. In other words, when a sixth of the population
of a nation which has undertaken to be the refuge
of liberty are slaves, and a whole country is unjustly
overrun and conquered by a foreign army, and
subjected to military law, I think that it is not too
soon for honest men to rebel and revolutionize.
What makes this duty the more urgent is the fact
that the country so overrun is not our own, but ours
is the invading army. . . .

Thoreau here describes Paley's political philosophy, which
reduces all civil obligation to "expediency."

But Paley appears never to have contemplated those
cases to which the rule of expediency does not
apply, in which a people, as well as an individual,
must do justice, cost what it may. If I have unjustly
wrested a plank from a drowning man, I must restore
it to him though I drown myself. This, according to
Paley, would be inconvenient. But he that would
save his life, in such a case, shall lose it. This
people must cease to hold slaves, and to make

war on Mexico, though it cost them their existence as a people.

In their practice, nations agree with Paley; but does any one think that Massachusetts does exactly what is right at the present crisis?
"A drab of state, a cloth-o'-silver slut,
To have her train borne up, and her soul trail in the dirt."

Practically speaking, the opponents to a reform in Massachusetts are not a hundred thousand politicians at the South, but a hundred thousand merchants and farmers here, who are more interested in commerce and agriculture than they are in humanity, and are not prepared to do justice to the slave and to Mexico, cost what it may. I quarrel not with far-off foes, but with those who, near at home, co-operate with, and do the bidding of those far away, and without whom the latter would be harmless. We are accustomed to say, that the mass of men are unprepared; but improvement is slow, because the few are not materially wiser or better than the many. It is not so important that many should be as good as you, as that there be some absolute goodness somewhere; for that will leaven the whole lump. There are thousands who are in opinion opposed to slavery and to the war, who yet in effect do nothing to put an end to them; who, esteeming themselves children of Washington and Franklin, sit down with their hands in *their pockets, and say that they know not what to do, and do nothing; who even postpone the question of freedom to the question of free-trade, and quietly read the prices-current along with the latest advices from Mexico, after dinner, and, it may be, fall asleep over them both. . . .*

All voting is a sort of gaming, like checkers or backgammon, with a slight moral tinge to it, a playing with right and wrong, with moral questions; and betting naturally accompanies it. The character of the voters is not staked. I cast my vote, perchance, as I think right; but I am not vitally concerned that that right should prevail. I am willing to leave it to the majority. Its obligation, therefore, never exceeds that of expediency. Even voting for the right is doing nothing for it. It is only expressing to men feebly your desire that it should prevail. A wise man will not leave the right to the mercy of chance, nor wish it to prevail through the power of the majority. There is but little virtue in the action of masses of men. When the majority shall at length vote for the abolition of slavery, it will be because they are indifferent to slavery, or because there is but little slavery left to be abolished by their vote. They will then be the only slaves. Only his vote can hasten the abolition of slavery who asserts his own freedom by his vote.

Thoreau here laments the lack of what he calls real "men" of independence and moral resolve.

It is not a man's duty, as a matter of course, to devote himself to the eradication of any, even the most enormous wrong; he may still properly have other concerns to engage him; but it is his duty, at least, to wash his hands of it, and, if he gives it no thought longer, not to give it practically his support. If I devote myself to other pursuits and contemplations, I must first see, at least, that I do not pursue them sitting upon another man's shoulders. I must get off him first, that he may pursue his contemplations too. See what gross inconsistency is tolerated. I have heard some of my townsmen say, "I should like to have them order me out to help put down an insurrection of the slaves, or to march to Mexico;—see if I would go"; and yet these very men have each, directly by their allegiance, and so indirectly, at least, by their money, furnished a substitute. The soldier is applauded who refuses to serve in an unjust war by those who do not refuse to sustain the unjust government which makes the war; is applauded by those whose own act and authority he disregards and sets at naught; as if the state were penitent to that degree that it hired one to scourge it while it sinned, but not to that degree that it left off sinning for a moment. Thus, under the name of Order and Civil Government, we are all made at last to pay homage to and support our own meanness. After the first blush of sin comes its indifference; and from immoral *it becomes, as it were, un*moral, *and not quite unnecessary to that life which we have made. . . .*

Thoreau states that disapproval of the state has to be acted on if it is to be worth anything.

Action from principle, the perception and the performance of right, changes things and relations; it is essentially revolutionary, and does not consist wholly with anything which was. It not only divides states and churches, it divides families; ay, it divides the individual, *separating the diabolical in him from the divine.*

Unjust laws exist: shall we be content to obey them, or shall we endeavor to amend them, and obey them until we have succeeded, or shall we transgress them at once? Men generally, under such a government as this, think that they ought to wait until they have persuaded the majority to alter them. They think that, if they should resist, the remedy would be worse than the evil. But it is the fault of the government itself that the remedy is *worse than the evil.* It *makes it worse. Why is it not more apt to anticipate and provide for reform? Why does it not cherish its wise minority? Why does it cry and resist before it is hurt? Why does it not encourage its citizens to be on the alert to point out its faults, and do better than it would have them? Why does it always crucify Christ, and excommunicate Copernicus and Luther, and pronounce Washington and Franklin rebels? . . .*

Thoreau allows some injustice to be part of the "machine of government," but if the machine is "of such a nature that it requires you to be an agent of injustice to another, then, I say, break the law."

As for adopting the ways which the State has provided for remedying the evil, I know not of such ways. They take too much time, and a man's life will be gone. I have other affairs to attend to. I came into this world, not chiefly to make this a good place to live in, but to live in it, be it good or bad. A man has not everything to do, but something; and because he cannot do everything, *it is not necessary that he should do* something *wrong. It is not my business to be petitioning the Governor or the Legislature any more than it is theirs to petition me; and if they should not hear my petition, what should I do then? But in this case the State has provided no way: its very Constitution is the evil. This may seem to be harsh and stubborn and unconciliatory; but it is to treat with the utmost kindness and consideration the only spirit that can appreciate or deserves it. So is all change for the better, like birth and death, which convulse the body.*

I do not hesitate to say, that those who call themselves Abolitionists should at once effectually withdraw their support, both in person and property, from the government of Massachusetts, and not wait till they constitute a majority of one, before they

> *suffer the right to prevail through them. I think that*
> *it is enough if they have God on their side, without*
> *waiting for that other one. Moreover, any man more*
> *right than his neighbors constitutes a majority of*
> *one already.*

Thoreau presents the nonpayment of taxes as the simplest form of resistance.

> *I know this well, that if one thousand, if one hundred,*
> *if ten men whom I could name—if ten honest men*
> *only—ay, if one HONEST man, in this State of*
> *Massachusetts, ceasing to hold slaves, were actually*
> *to withdraw from this copartnership, and be locked*
> *up in the county jail therefor, it would be the abolition*
> *of slavery in America. For it matters not how small the*
> *beginning may seem to be: what is once well done is*
> *done forever. . . .*

But, says Thoreau, there is more talk than action.

> *Under a government which imprisons any unjustly,*
> *the true place for a just man is also a prison.*
> *The proper place to-day, the only place which*
> *Massachusetts has provided for her freer and less*
> *desponding spirits, is in her prisons, to be put out and*
> *locked out of the State by her own act, as they have*
> *already put themselves out by their principles. It is*
> *there that the fugitive slave, and the Mexican prisoner*
> *on parole, and the Indian come to plead the wrongs of*
> *his race should find them; on that separate, but more*
> *free and honorable ground, where the State places*

those who are not with her, but against her—the only
house in a slave State in which a free man can abide
with honor. If any think that their influence would be
lost there, and their voices no longer afflict the ear of
the State, that they would not be as an enemy within
its walls, they do not know by how much truth is
stronger than error, nor how much more eloquently
and effectively he can combat injustice who has
experienced a little in his own person. Cast your
whole vote, not a strip of paper merely, but your
whole influence. A minority is powerless while it
conforms to the majority; it is not even a minority
then; but it is irresistible when it clogs by its whole
weight. If the alternative is to keep all just men in
prison, or give up war and slavery, the State will not
hesitate which to choose. If a thousand men were
not to pay their tax-bills this year, that would not be
a violent and bloody measure, as it would be to pay
them, and enable the State to commit violence and
shed innocent blood. This is, in fact, the definition of
a peaceable revolution, if any such is possible. If the
tax-gatherer, or any other public officer, asks me, as
one has done, "But what shall I do?" my answer is,
"If you really wish to do anything, resign your office."
When the subject has refused allegiance, and the
officer has resigned his office, then the revolution is
accomplished. But even suppose blood should flow. Is
there not a sort of blood shed when the conscience is

wounded? Through this wound a man's real manhood
and immortality flow out, and he bleeds to an
everlasting death. I see this blood flowing now. . . .

Thoreau now moves on to discuss the conflict between
justice and wealth.

Absolutely speaking, the more money, the less virtue;
for money comes between a man and his objects, and
obtains them for him; and it was certainly no great
virtue to obtain it. It puts to rest many questions
which he would otherwise be taxed to answer; while
the only new question which it puts is the hard but
superfluous one, how to spend it. Thus his moral
ground is taken from under his feet. The opportunities
of living are diminished in proportion as what are
called the "means" are increased. The best thing
a man can do for his culture when he is rich is to
endeavor to carry out those schemes which he
entertained when he was poor. . . .

He quotes Christ, saying render to Caesar what is Caesar's
and to God what is God's.

When I converse with the freest of my neighbors,
I perceive that, whatever they may say about the
magnitude and seriousness of the question, and their
regard for the public tranquillity, the long and the
short of the matter is, that they cannot spare the
protection of the existing government, and they dread
the consequences to their property and families of
disobedience to it. For my own part, I should not like

to think that I ever rely on the protection of the State.
But, if I deny the authority of the State when it
presents its tax-bill, it will soon take and waste all my
property, and so harass me and my children without
end. This is hard. This makes it impossible for a man
to live honestly, and at the same time comfortably, in
outward respects. It will not be worth the while to
accumulate property; that would be sure to go again.
You must hire or squat somewhere, and raise but a
small crop, and eat that soon. You must live within
yourself, and depend upon yourself always tucked up
and ready for a start, and not have many affairs. A
man may grow rich in Turkey even, if he will be in all
respects a good subject of the Turkish government.
Confucius said: "If a state is governed by the
principles of reason, poverty and misery are subjects
of shame; if a state is not governed by the principles
of reason, riches and honors are the subjects of
shame." No: until I want the protection of
Massachusetts to be extended to me in some distant
Southern port, where my liberty is endangered, or
until I am bent solely on building up an estate at
home by peaceful enterprise, I can afford to refuse
allegiance to Massachusetts, and her right to my
property and life. It costs me less in every sense to
incur the penalty of disobedience to the State than
it would to obey. I should feel as if I were worth less
in that case. . . .

Thoreau now documents his nonpayment of taxes toward the Church and his agreement with the state that, because he was not a member of the Church, he should not pay toward it. Then he briefly describes his night in jail and its ineffectiveness in punishing his body while his mind remained free.

Thus the State never intentionally confronts a man's sense, intellectual or moral, but only his body, his senses. It is not armed with superior wit or honesty, but with superior physical strength. I was not born to be forced. I will breathe after my own fashion. Let us see who is the strongest. What force has a multitude? They only can force me who obey a higher law than I. They force me to become like themselves. I do not hear of men *being* forced *to live this way or that by masses of men. What sort of life were that to live? When I meet a government which says to me, "Your money or your life," why should I be in haste to give it my money? It may be in a great strait, and not know what to do: I cannot help that. It must help itself; do as I do. It is not worth the while to snivel about it. I am not responsible for the successful working of the machinery of society. I am not the son of the engineer. I perceive that, when an acorn and a chestnut fall side by side, the one does not remain inert to make way for the other, but both obey their own laws, and spring and grow and flourish as best they can, till one, perchance, overshadows and*

destroys the other. If a plant cannot live according
to its nature, it dies; and so a man.

Thoreau now goes on to describe his night in prison and his conversations with his fellow prisoner.

It was like travelling into a far country, such as I had
never expected to behold, to lie there for one night. It
seemed to me that I never had heard the town-clock
strike before, nor the evening sounds of the village;
for we slept with the windows open, which were
inside the grating. It was to see my native village in
the light of the Middle Ages, and our Concord was
turned into a Rhine stream, and visions of knights
and castles passed before me. They were the voices
of old burghers that I heard in the streets. I was an
involuntary spectator and auditor of whatever was
done and said in the kitchen of the adjacent village-
inn—a wholly new and rare experience to me. It was
a closer view of my native town. I was fairly inside of
it. I never had seen its institutions before. This is one
of its peculiar institutions; for it is a shire town. I began
to comprehend what its inhabitants were about. . . .

The following day they have breakfast, the other prisoner leaves for work in the fields, and Thoreau is released.

When I came out of prison—for some one interfered,
and paid that tax—I did not perceive that great
changes had taken place on the common, such as
he observed who went in a youth and emerged a
tottering and gray-headed man; and yet a change

had to my eyes come over the scene—the town, and State, and country, greater than any that mere time could effect. I saw yet more distinctly the State in which I lived. I saw to what extent the people among whom I lived could be trusted as good neighbors and friends; that their friendship was for summer weather only; that they did not greatly propose to do right; that they were a distinct race from me by their prejudices and superstitions, as the Chinamen and Malays are; that in their sacrifices to humanity they ran no risks, not even to their property; that after all they were not so noble but they treated the thief as he had treated them, and hoped, by a certain outward observance and a few prayers, and by walking in a particular straight though useless path from time to time, to save their souls. This may be to judge my neighbors harshly; for I believe that many of them are not aware that they have such an institution as the jail in their village.

It was formerly the custom in our village, when a poor debtor came out of jail, for his acquaintances to salute him, looking through their fingers, which were crossed to represent the grating of a jail window, "How do ye do?" My neighbors did not thus salute me, but first looked at me, and then at one another, as if I had returned from a long journey. I was put into jail as I was going to the shoemaker's to get a shoe which was mended. When I was let out the next morning, I proceeded to finish my errand, and, having put on my mended shoe, joined a huckleberry party, who were impatient to put themselves under my conduct; and in half an hour—for the horse was soon tackled—was in the midst of a huckleberry field, on one of our highest hills, two miles off, and then the State was nowhere to be seen.

This is the whole history of "My Prisons."

I have never declined paying the highway tax, because I am as desirous of being a good neighbor as I am of being a bad subject; and as for supporting schools, I am doing my part to educate my fellow-countrymen now. It is for no particular item in the tax-bill that I refuse to pay it. I simply wish to refuse allegiance to the State, to withdraw and stand aloof from it effectually. I do not care to trace the course of my dollar, if I could, till it buys a man or a musket to shoot one with—the dollar is innocent—but I am concerned to trace the effects of my allegiance. In fact, I quietly declare war with the State, after my fashion, though I will still make what use and get what advantage of her I can, as is usual in such cases.

If others pay the tax which is demanded of me, from a sympathy with the State, they do but what they have already done in their own case, or rather they abet injustice to a greater extent than the State requires. If they pay the tax from a mistaken interest

in the individual taxed, to save his property, or
prevent his going to jail, it is because they have
not considered wisely how far they let their private
feelings interfere with the public good.

This, then, is my position at present. But one
cannot be too much on his guard in such a case, lest
his action be biased by obstinacy or an undue regard
for the opinions of men. Let him see that he does only
what belongs to himself and to the hour.

Thoreau now draws a distinction between the natural
elements, which it is futile to resist, and the state, which
although a similar brute force, is man-made and therefore
requires to be resisted at times. He has no desire to obstruct
the government more than is necessary.

Seen from a lower point of view, the Constitution, with
all its faults, is very good; the law and the courts are
very respectable; even this State and this American
government are, in many respects, very admirable,
and rare things, to be thankful for, such as a great
many have described them; but seen from a point of
view a little higher, they are what I have described
them; seen from a higher still, and the highest, who
shall say what they are, or that they are worth looking
at or thinking of at all?

However, the government does not concern
me much, and I shall bestow the fewest possible
thoughts on it. It is not many moments that I live under
a government, even in this world. If a man is thought-

free, fancy-free, imagination-free, that which is not
never for a long time appearing to be to him, unwise
rulers or reformers cannot fatally interrupt him.

I know that most men think differently from
myself; but those whose lives are by profession
devoted to the study of these or kindred subjects
content me as little as any. Statesmen and legislators,
standing so completely within the institution,
never distinctly and nakedly behold it. They speak
of moving society, but have no resting-place without
it. They may be men of a certain experience and
discrimination, and have no doubt invented ingenious
and even useful systems, for which we sincerely
thank them; but all their wit and usefulness lie
within certain not very wide limits. They are wont
to forget that the world is not governed by
policy and expediency.

Thoreau introduces Daniel Webster, a senator for Massachusetts, as a sensible and practical politician, but one who is unable or unwilling to rise above the political process and consider an issue from the standpoint of truth.

They who know of no purer sources of truth, who
have traced up its stream no higher, stand, and wisely
stand, by the Bible and the Constitution, and drink at
it there with reverence and humility; but they who
behold where it comes trickling into this lake or that
pool, gird up their loins once more, and continue their
pilgrimage toward its fountainhead.

No man with a genius for legislation has appeared in America. They are rare in the history of the world. There are orators, politicians, and eloquent men, by the thousand; but the speaker has not yet opened his mouth to speak who is capable of settling the much-vexed questions of the day. We love eloquence for its own sake, and not for any truth which it may utter, or any heroism it may inspire. Our legislators have not yet learned the comparative value of free-trade and of freedom, of union, and of rectitude, to a nation. They have no genius or talent for comparatively humble questions of taxation and finance, commerce and manufacturers and agriculture. If we were left solely to the wordy wit of legislators in Congress for our guidance, uncorrected by the seasonable experience and the effectual complaints of the people, America would not long retain her rank among the nations. For eighteen hundred years, though perchance I have no right to say it, the New Testament has been written; yet where is the legislator who has wisdom and practical talent enough to avail himself of the light which it sheds on the science of legislation?

The authority of government, even such as I am willing to submit to—for I will cheerfully obey those who know and can do better than I, and in many things even those who neither know nor can do so well—is still an impure one: to be strictly just, it must have the sanction and consent of the governed. It can have no pure right over my person and property but what I concede to it. The progress from an absolute to a limited monarchy, from a limited monarchy to a democracy, is a progress toward a true respect for the individual. Even the Chinese philosopher was wise enough to regard the individual as the basis of the empire. Is a democracy, such as we know it, the last improvement possible in government? Is it not possible to take a step further towards recognizing and organizing the rights of man? There will never be a really free and enlightened State until the State comes to recognize the individual as a higher and independent power, from which all its own power and authority are derived, and treats him accordingly. I please myself with imagining a State at least which can afford to be just to all men, and to treat the individual with respect as a neighbor; which even would not think it inconsistent with its own repose if a few were to live aloof from it, not meddling with it, nor embraced by it, who fulfilled all the duties of neighbors and fellow-men. A State which bore this kind of fruit, and suffered it to drop off as fast as it ripened, would prepare the way for a still more perfect and glorious State, which also I have imagined, but not yet anywhere seen.

The immediate impact of Thoreau's text might be summed up quite simply: There was none. If you wanted an exemplar of the saying that a prophet has no honor in his own country, you could do worse than choose Thoreau. Ignored throughout the nineteenth century and into the twentieth, Thoreau's work came to the attention of a wide public in the United States only from about the 1920s. Even then he was known chiefly as a celebrator of the natural wilderness and a Romantic advocate of self-reliance and "getting back to nature." As we shall see in the next section of this book, his influence as a political thinker, although significant in Europe and India, was negligible in the United States until the radical movements of the 1960s brought his essay to prominence.

Thoreau's early reputation in America was as a naturalist, and his books were produced in deluxe coffee table editions more suited to be looked at and admired than read. Of Thoreau the reformer there was no sign.

There are several clear reasons why Thoreau's work was not taken up immediately. They fall into three main areas: the nature of the message, the perception of Thoreau as a person, and his publication history.

The Message of "Civil Disobedience"

Perhaps the most obvious reason Thoreau's lecture did not produce an identifiable response was that it did not propose a specific kind of action. There was no program of reform outlined, no call to band together as a group or party around an issue. His opposition to the Mexican War and to the return of runaway slaves to the South were both uncontroversial views to the audience he was addressing in Concord, although his opposition to the rule of law would not have been widely shared. In any case, by January 1848 the Mexican War was nearing its end, which suggests that Thoreau's aims were something other than immediate action. True, he did suggest that all the citizens of Massachusetts should cease paying their taxes forthwith, but this was more a goad to complacency than a prescription for reform.

The issue of slavery had been coming to a crisis for some twenty years before Thoreau gave his lecture, and the Compromise of 1850 was too unpopular to offer much hope of a lasting resolution.

The lecture, as was true of much of Thoreau's work, was a challenge rather than a program. Thoreau was a prophet, in the sense that he was pointing to a fundamental truth or principle that he believed was being neglected by the people at large. He was not a politician, in the sense of having a clear policy on what to do about it. "Civil Disobedience" was an invitation to people to think for themselves, to act in accordance with the demands of their consciences, and to take account of the "supreme law," the "higher truth" as expressed by the Transcendentalist worldview. These are not ideas that translate readily into policy documents or 12-point plans. At the beginning of *Walden*, Thoreau set out his aim as "to brag as lustily as chanticleer in the morning, standing on his roost, if only to wake my neighbors up." Thoreau was planting a seed. The reason it took that seed so long to germinate is considered in the following sections.

Thoreau's Personality

The second reason for the neglect of Thoreau was the view of the man and his work offered by contemporary reviews and journalism. Reviews of his book *Walden* were in the main positive, one describing it as a "prose poem [of] classical elegance, and New England homeliness, with a sprinkle of Oriental magnificence in it"; another reviewer remarked "We do not get such a book every day, or often in a century." However, there were some consistent themes in the reviews that offered a not entirely sympathetic view of Thoreau's character. Many remarked on the conflicts in his work between philosophy and practicality, individualism and social responsibility, physical isolation and social involvement: The overall picture is of a somewhat rarefied, idealized, intellectually self-absorbed vision of the world, a moralizer looking on at the doings of his fellow men with a degree of Olympian detachment. The *Boston Atlas* observed that, far from showing himself at one with his readers in common humanity, Thoreau "fondly deems himself emancipated from this thraldom, and looks down upon them as an inferior tribe."

Allied to these complaints was the accusation of hypocrisy on Thoreau's part. His withdrawal to the woods described in *Walden* was derided in some quarters as being little more than a charade. If it was so wonderful in the

Thoreau's sojourn at Walden Pond was not merely a pastoral idyll. In a famous passage in *Walden* he expresses his admiration for the technological wonder of the railroad that he can hear from his hut. Thoreau does not reject industrial progress, but he challenges the reader to see it as a means and not an end in itself.

woods, asked one reviewer, why didn't he stay there rather than coming back after two years? It was all very well to criticize commercial enterprise, accumulation of wealth, and the rush and hurry of the social world, when he had "borrowed the cunning tools and manufactured products of civilization, to enable him to endure the wilderness . . . . He only played savage on the borders of civilization; going back to the quiet town whenever he was unable to supply his civilized wants by his own powers." In short, Thoreau was a sanctimonious humbug, biting the hand that he was happy to allow to feed him once he got back from his sojourn in the woods.

Reviews of *Aesthetic Papers*, in which "Civil Disobedience" was first published, were hostile to his views and shared some of the characteristics noted above. The *Boston Courier*, a newspaper that was supportive of the government's Mexican War, said "We must dismiss Mr. Thoreau with the earnest prayer that he may become a better subject in time," and suggested that he should take his preaching to the red republicans in France. Another review remarked that Thoreau would make it "every man's duty to refuse allegiance to the state whenever any of its laws violate his conscience"—a gross misrepresentation of what Thoreau actually says—and points out that he appeals

James Russell Lowell was the epitome of the patrician American man of letters. Nonetheless, Thoreau's biographer Henry Salt denounced Lowell's essay on Thoreau thirty years after its publication as a "masterpiece of hostile innuendo."

to the New Testament, or "that part of it which may be made to coincide with his own opinions," again suggesting a degree of hypocrisy on the author's part. The response was no better when Thoreau's essay was published in book form in 1866. *The Christian Register* described it as an exercise in "impracticable and half-insane theorizing," while the *Philadelphia Enquirer* dismissed it as a "sententious diatribe."

The view of Thoreau as a dry, humorless, stoic, and aloof idealist was fixed in the public mind by two essays published by critics after his death. James Russell Lowell was professor of modern languages and literature at Harvard and an almost exact contemporary of Thoreau. He had written "The Biglow Papers," a satiric attack on the proslavery party and the government, soon after the beginning of the Mexican War, and was the most renowned literary critic in America when he wrote a review of Thoreau's letters in the *North American Review* in October 1865. In this piece he paid tribute to Emerson as the source of an American culture and aesthetics independent of English thought, and claimed that "if it was ever questionable whether democracy could develop a gentleman, the problem has been affirmatively solved at last." He was less complimentary about Thoreau, describing him as a conceited, humorless crank, forever claiming an originality of thought and idea that was nothing more than the pursuit of perversity and paradox for its own sake, and entirely lacking in the artistic power required to shape a work to completion. Lowell ridiculed Thoreau's celebration of nature and the natural law as sentimental primitivism, and attacked his misanthropy: "A greater familiarity with ordinary men would have done Thoreau good, by showing him how many fine qualities were common to the race." Once more the charge of hypocrisy appears:

He squatted on another man's land; he borrows an
axe; his boards, his nails, his bricks, his mortar, his
books, his lamp, his fish-hooks, his plough, his hoe,
all turn state's evidence against him as an
accomplice in the sin of that artificial civilization
which rendered it possible that such a person as
Henry D. Thoreau should exist at all.

Lowell, who later became American minister in Spain and then in England, also condemned Thoreau's distaste for political engagement:

While he studied with respectful attention the minks
and woodchucks, his neighbors, he looked with
utter contempt on the august drama of destiny
of which his country was the scene, and on which
the curtain had already risen.

Lowell's disparagement has been seen as a peevish response to Thoreau's attack on the kind of genteel and civilized values that Lowell himself exemplified. And by "drama of destiny," he was evidently referring to the "manifest destiny" of the exploitation of the West, the brutal and imperialist

An ambrotype image of Thoreau from 1861 shows the effects of ill-health. He was only 44 when this picture was taken, but the change in the five years since the 1856 daguerreotype (*see page 6*) is striking.

aspects of which Thoreau foresaw two generations before their occurrence. Nonetheless, the essay was instrumental in forming a common view of the man and his works.

The Truth about Thoreau

Many of the accusations made against Thoreau in these various appraisals are readily answered from close reading of what he actually wrote. *Walden* has numerous instances in which Thoreau exhorts his readers to think for themselves: "I would not have anyone adopt my mode of living on any account"; he did ally himself with his fellows ("I brag for humanity rather than for myself"); and his intention was not to hold himself up as superior, but to show by example the importance of examining how we live and attending to the "divinity in man": "Not until we have lost the world do we begin to find ourselves, and realize where we are and the infinite extent of our relations." He gave his reason for coming back from Walden woods as having "several more lives to live, and [I] could not spare any more time for that one."

Even the accusation about wanting to undermine society and civil government while enjoying its benefits can be answered in his own words. In the first place, he says in "Civil Disobedience" that only important issues should be addressed by refusal to obey the law; what he calls mere "friction" in the machinery of government is not worth worrying about. In the second place, Thoreau does not throw out the idea of legitimate government altogether. He was not an anarchist and never joined any anarchist group. (As far as we know, he never joined any political group at all; even though he had sympathies with the Garrisonian abolitionists and came from an abolitionist family, he was not a member of Garrison's organization.) His essay famously begins with the motto "That government is best which governs not at all," but in the context of the essay as a whole this is a millennial hope rather than a concrete proposal. Thoreau says that when humanity has reached a point of perfectibility that allows each person to act in conformity with the higher law, there will be no need for any government. Until that happens, he is happy to consent to the rule of law, but not at any cost. His statement of this position shows a nice line in self-mockery: "I quietly declare war with the State, after my fashion, though I will still make what use and get what advantage of her I can, as is usual in such cases." That is to say, you can make a pragmatic decision to cooperate with the state and its legal requirements in most day-to-day matters, but that does not mean that you may not withhold allegiance when a serious moral principle is at stake.

A close reading of Thoreau's words was unlikely to have been encouraged by a second and much more significant essay, however. Published in the *Atlantic Monthly* magazine in August 1862, it was an elaboration of the eulogy delivered at Thoreau's funeral by his mentor, Emerson. Emerson begins with some biographical facts before offering a brief sketch of his friend's character:

He was bred to no profession; he never married; he lived alone; he never went to church; he never voted . . . he ate no flesh, he drank no wine, he never knew the use of tobacco . . . he had no talent for wealth, and knew how to be poor without the least hint of squalor or inelegance . . . . He had no temptation to fight against; no appetites, no passions, no taste for elegant trifles.

Given the odor of bloodless sanctity that hangs around this portrait, it is little surprise to find that Thoreau had few intimate friends:

It seemed that as if his first instinct on hearing a proposition was to controvert it, so impatient was he of the limitations of our daily thought . . . . Hence no equal companion stood in affectionate relations with one so pure and guileless. "I love Henry," said one of his friends, "but I cannot like him; and as for taking his arm, I should as soon think of taking the arm of an elm tree."

Emerson is being coy here, for the friend in question was none other than Emerson himself, and the comment about the elm tree appears in his journal.

Emerson also draws attention to Thoreau's habit of judging all things by the measure of Concord, his home village, which he claims as the "playful expression of his conviction of the indifference of all places, and that the best place for each is where he stands," but which strikes the reader as being absurdly parochial. Finally Emerson betrays a degree of frustration with Thoreau's apparent disengagement: "I so much regret the loss of his rare powers of action, that I cannot help counting it a fault in him that he had no ambition. Wanting this, instead of engineering for all America, he was the captain of a huckleberry party."

Perhaps the most astonishing feature of the essay is the fact that Thoreau's writing is barely touched on. Emerson makes no mention of Thoreau's literary career, he offers no evaluation of his published works, and the only writing that he does quote is taken from the unpublished journal, reinforcing the idea that Thoreau wrote only for himself. The picture that emerges is of an obsessive, antisocial, parochial, ascetic hermit. As an act of professional and personal betrayal, it would be hard to improve on this performance.

The source of the unsympathetic (some might say hostile) tone of the funeral address lay in the estrangement that had arisen between the two men by about 1849, which we looked at in an earlier chapter. The local audience would probably have known of the quarrel and would have judged Emerson's remarks accordingly. Louisa May Alcott, who attended the funeral, remarked in a letter to a friend that the address was "not appropriate to the time or place." However, the memoir had a much wider readership than the merely local, serving as the introduction to the two major editions of Thoreau's works that appeared in the century after his death, as well as being widely anthologized and reprinted to this

Louisa May Alcott regretted the tone of Emerson's funeral address, but nonetheless the Emersonian version of Thoreau was the one that came to be the accepted view.

A WEEK ON THE CONCORD
AND MERRIMACK
RIVERS

BY

HENRY DAVID THOREAU

BOSTON AND NEW YORK
HOUGHTON MIFFLIN COMPANY
The Riverside Press Cambridge

In 1853 Thoreau noted in his *Journal* that he had a library of 900 volumes, 700 of which he had written himself, a self-deprecating reference to the unsold copies of *A Week* that the publisher had returned to him.

day. Readers coming to the essay without a knowledge of the context would be far more likely to take it at face value; Emerson was one of the great figures of nineteenth-century American culture and a man whose opinions therefore carried some weight. Thoreau was not around to defend himself. It would be almost impossible to exaggerate the damage that Emerson's essay did to Thoreau's contemporary reputation, or the hindrance that the myth of Thoreau as a minor figure who squandered his talents was to his finding an appreciative readership in the decades after his death.

Thoreau's Publishing History

The final reason for Thoreau's neglect is the mundane one that to be read, you have to be published. Thoreau's first book, *A Week on the Concord and Merrimack Rivers*, was published in 1849 at his own expense, as was the practice at the time. It was poorly publicized, however, and sold only about a fifth of the print run, leaving Thoreau with a large debt. His second book, *Walden*, published in 1854, was more successful, but this was the last book Thoreau published. Quarrels with editors over the editing of his essays meant that none was published in book form during his lifetime. Bearing in mind that the collected edition of his works published in 1906 ran to 20 volumes, there was a great deal of writing that Thoreau never got around to publishing, other than in magazines. "Resistance to Civil Government" was published in *Aesthetic Papers*, but this periodical attracted little interest, and the first issue proved to be the only one. Fortunately, after Thoreau's death his friends and admirers put considerable efforts into editing and publishing the material that Thoreau had bequeathed. Several volumes of essays came out during the 1860s, but although they kept Thoreau's name alive, sales were unspectacular. A surge of interest in nature writing in the 1880s led Houghton Mifflin to publish some selections from Thoreau's *Journals* as *Early Spring in Massachusetts*. This was followed by three volumes for the other seasons, and Thoreau began to acquire a larger readership. A collected edition in 10 volumes was published in 1892, and then the 20-volume edition, including 14 volumes of the *Journals*, came out in 1906. Even if interest in Thoreau was slow to spread, his works were now at least available to the public. Nonetheless, where he was known in his own country it was as a nature writer and a proponent of the simple life. Appreciation of his importance as a political thinker came from a quarter that Thoreau himself, given his quarrels with Emerson, might well have found disheartening—England.

Thoreau and the English Socialists

Whereas in the United States Thoreau was being swamped by a tide of *ad hominem* invective, or else domesticated as an environmentalist *avant la lettre*, in England his political thought was embraced by elements of the nascent Socialist movement. As with so many well-known facts about Thoreau, this aspect of his impact has been variously misunderstood and overstated. One of Thoreau's biographers of the early twentieth century stated candidly that the "British Labour Party, offspring of William Morris and Marx, used *Walden* as a pocket-piece and travelling Bible of their faith," and another writer spoke of Thoreau's "enormous influence" on the British Labour movement. Although it is true to say that Thoreau achieved prominence in England long before he had any such reputation in America, his influence was not as widespread as might be thought from these quotations.

Part of the reason for this misunderstanding might be the complexity of Socialist politics in late Victorian England. Socialism had begun in England with the co-operative movement of Robert Owen in the early nineteenth century, and was continued by the revolutionary Chartists in the 1850s. However, by the 1880s the situation was complicated by the existence of a number of factions, with different emphases. The Social Democratic Foundation (SDF), founded in 1881, was led by H.M. Hyndman, who was a Marxist, although his interpretations of Marxism were displeasing to Marx himself. The Socialist League formed as

William Morris, one of the great action men of Victorian Britain, had little time for what he regarded as Thoreau's detachment from the struggle and flurry of social life.

a breakaway movement from the SDF in 1884, under the leadership of William Morris, who was less a Marxist than an ethical Socialist, concerned as much with the quality of life that Socialism promised as with the struggle between capital and labor. There was also the Fabian Society, a grouping of middle-class intellectuals under the influence of Beatrice and Sidney Webb, and other smaller groups such as the Fellowship of the New Life and the Anglican Guild of St. Matthew. In 1893 the working-class Independent Labour Party was formed. These groups were frequently in conflict with each other as much as with the common enemy, capitalism. Thus, the SDF was in favor of achieving working-class representation in Parliament, whereas the Socialist League viewed Parliament as a corrupt and worthless institution, and was eventually taken over by the anarchists, who rejected democratic processes in favor of violent action. In short, English "Socialism" was a many-headed beast, and it would therefore be difficult to claim that any one thinker could hold sway over all its different factions.

There is no evidence that William Morris was influenced by Thoreau (he is not mentioned in the most recent biography of Morris). Morris read *Walden* but he considered Thoreau to be too much of a spectator of human life and insufficiently involved on behalf of his fellows:

> *I know from experience what a comfortable life one might lead if one could be careful not to concern oneself with* persons *but with* things; *or persons in the light of things. But nature won't allow it . . . .*

Morris's Socialist League was just one of many factions in the British Labour movement. This photograph, taken in the garden of Morris's house, includes Morris himself and his wife and daughter.

Henry George's book *Progress and Poverty*, published in 1879, became one of the most widely read works on political economy. His arguments in favor of land nationalization and a single tax on property to replace taxes on capital and labor were influential on radical thinkers in Europe.

Nor is there any indication of Thoreauvian influence on the Webbs or Hyndman. A more significant American figure might be found in Henry George, whose book *Progress and Poverty* was read by many of the leading Socialists of the time, and who undertook lecture tours of England in 1882 and 1883. Nonetheless, a more focused examination does reveal three important individuals in Socialist politics who definitely engaged with Thoreau's political ideas, one of whom played a significant role in putting Thoreau onto the world stage.

Robert Blatchford and Edward Carpenter

Robert Blatchford was a journalist who was converted to Socialism in 1889 after reading *A Summary of the Principles of Socialism* by Hyndman and Morris, and was later a founder of the Independent Labour Party. His weekly columns in the Manchester *Sunday Chronicle*—and later in his own newspaper, *The Clarion*—did a great deal to popularize the idea of Socialism among the English working classes. Blatchford had read *Walden*, and Thoreau's ideas about simplicity of life and the quest for a more "spiritual" dimension to human existence chimed in with his own Socialist beliefs. In 1893 he published a book, *Merrie England*, offering his view of why Socialism was necessary and the kind of world it might produce. Echoes of Thoreau can be found throughout his book:

> *A life which consists of nothing but eating, and drinking, and working is not a human life—it is the life of a beast. Such a life is not worth living. If we*

are to spend all our days and nights in a kind of
penal servitude, continually toiling and suffering in
order to live, we had better break at once the chains
of our bitter slavery and die.

Merrie England was dismissed in some quarters as hopelessly impressionistic and lacking in political sophistication (the future Labour leader Ramsay MacDonald said it was like a man explaining a motorcar by describing a wheelbarrow), but it sold more than two million copies in a penny edition and was instrumental in recruiting sympathizers to Socialism. Blatchford recommended *Walden* to his readers, and so introduced Thoreau to a wide English public.

Edward Carpenter came from a comfortable middle-class family and was educated at Cambridge University, where he became a fellow of Trinity Hall and took holy orders. However, Carpenter's Romantic and individualist temperament was soon in conflict with the stifling conformity of late Victorian Cambridge. In 1874 he resigned his fellowship and began lecturing in the north of England as part of the University Extension Scheme, which was aimed at the education of women and working men. His teaching brought him into contact with working-class life, and stimulated his ideas on human freedom and equality, which culminated in his Whitmanesque prose poem *Towards Democracy*, published in 1883. In the same year, with an inheritance from his father, he bought some land at Millthorpe near Sheffield, where he adopted a primitive communist lifestyle with a small group of working men and women. Carpenter had read

The Clarion was a weekly newspaper founded by Robert Blatchford in 1891. Its colloquial, populist style was aimed at bringing Socialist ideas to the attention of the working classes, and *Merrie England* was serialized in the paper before being published as a book.

**TOWARDS
DEMOCRACY**

(1915)

Edward Carpenter

Millthorpe, in the north of England, was a Socialist Utopian commune established by Edward Carpenter, with similarities to the American Transcendentalist communal experiments such as Brook Farm. *Towards Democracy* expressed Carpenter's small-scale ideal of Socialist life.

Thoreau's books and was impressed by his ideas (he sent a copy of *Walden* to Morris and made a pilgrimage to Walden Pond in 1884). The Thoreauvian influence is clear in the style of living that Carpenter adopted and in the quotations from Thoreau that appear throughout his writings.

Carpenter knew many of the leading Socialist figures of the time, such as Hyndman and Morris, and he funded the publication of the SDF journal *Justice* and later joined Morris's Socialist League. He lectured and wrote essays in support of numerous progressive causes, including women's rights, sexual reform, and industrial reorganization. *Towards Democracy* was reprinted many times, becoming a Bible for many young radicals. He also wrote the Socialist hymn "England Arise!," which was being sung at meetings of the Young Communist League in London as late as the mid-1960s. Freedom of the individual was as paramount for Carpenter as for Thoreau, and his version of Socialism was focused on small local groups and the self-realization of each person. Although he was supportive of Blatchford's Independent Labour Party, Carpenter withdrew increasingly from Socialist politics as it evolved into a national movement. Nonetheless, in his revolt against middle-class respectability (his vegetarianism, his wearing of sandals, and his open homosexuality scandalized bourgeois society), Carpenter was an important symbol of individual freedom not only for contemporaries but also for later writers, such as E.M. Forster and D.H. Lawrence.

Edward Carpenter, photographed at Millthorpe in 1905. Carpenter, like Thoreau, has been seen as a reclusive and eccentric figure, but his ideal of a Socialism that encompassed sexual and social freedom as well as material equality won him many followers.

Henry Salt

The most important of the three English Socialist devotees of Thoreau was Henry Salt. Like Carpenter, Salt started his professional life in a bastion of the English establishment, Eton College, where he was a master. However, within a few years of arriving at Eton, Salt began to question the values of the world in which he moved, finding that few students were interested in intellectual matters, that new ideas were effectively banned at Eton, and that the governing principle of life there was respectability. Salt's brother-in-law, J.L. Joynes, had also been a master at Eton, but had been obliged to resign after publishing a pamphlet describing his arrest in Ireland for inciting public disorder while accompanying the American Henry George at one of his lectures. Joynes had become a prominent member of the SDF and introduced Salt to a number of leading Socialists, such as Morris, Hyndman, Eleanor Marx, and Carpenter. Salt read Carpenter's essays and was thus introduced to Thoreau's work—and to the idea of simplicity of life. In his autobiography he wrote of discovering that

> it was possible to dispense with the greater part of
> the trappings with which we are encumbered, and to
> live far more simply and cheaply than was dreamed
> of in polite society.

Salt resigned from his job at Eton and retired to a cottage in Surrey, where he began a serious reading of Thoreau. One of his visitors was W.J. Jupp, an ardent Thoreauvian who had devoted a chapter of his autobiography, *The Wayfarer*, to

When Gandhi attended a meeting of the Vegetarian Society in London in 1931, Salt was given the place of honor on his right in recognition of the inspiration that the young Gandhi had found in his books.

Thoreau, not only remarking on his qualities as a naturalist but also characterizing him as a "relentless Thinker and searcher for truth." Jupp was a charter member of the Fellowship of the New Life—more a Transcendentalist than a Socialist group—which insisted on the necessity of moral as well as political and economic reform of society— ideas that can be closely linked to Thoreau's reform writings. Salt's brother-in-law Joynes was also a member of the Fellowship, and thus Salt was encouraged in his study of Thoreau's work.

Salt's first published writing on Thoreau appeared in the SDF journal, *Justice*, in 1885. He gave an account of Thoreau's career and his book *Walden*, and praised Thoreau's reformist principles:

> *Among those American writers who have denounced the anomalies and tyrannies of Transatlantic government and society, none have done so more eloquently than Henry Thoreau. Though not a professed Socialist, but appealing rather to the individual capabilities of man, Thoreau deserves to be studied by every social reformer . . . .*

Powerful in its advocacy of Thoreau as this article was, there is no evidence, as we have seen, that the SDF or its leader Hyndman took much notice. Perhaps it is not surprising. The SDF saw its role solely in Marxist materialist terms, and its chief objective was collective political action toward economic reform in favor of the working classes. Thoreau was perhaps too much of an individualist to appeal to this

Salt's withdrawal to a cottage in Surrey in the south of England allowed him time to think and write, and his two-volume autobiography reflects a lifetime's support for a number of progressive causes.

wing of the English reformers. Certainly, Salt began to move away from doctrinaire Socialism, taking a much broader view of Thoreau's relevance for the reform movement.

A second essay in 1886 examined Thoreau's main philosophical ideas, related to the "perfectibility of man" and the importance of the individual. This essay also drew attention explicitly to the importance of "Civil Disobedience." Salt decided that what was needed was a proper biography of Thoreau, and to gain information he wrote to people in America who had known Thoreau personally or who were familiar with his work. Salt's aim in writing his book, as he declared in a letter to Daniel Ricketson, a friend of Thoreau, was

interpreting *rather than criticising in the ordinary sense, it being my belief that in the case of such a real man of genius as Thoreau, it is the duty of the critic to accept him thankfully, and not to carp unduly at his limitations.*

Salt's biography, published in 1890, certainly took into account Thoreau's failings and defects of character, but unlike his American counterparts Salt also gave a sympathetic appraisal of Thoreau's ideas. He presented Thoreau as a deliberate artist, contradicting Lowell's picture of him as a bits-and-pieces writer, and gave due weight to Thoreau's writing style, his humor, and his love of paradox. He distinguished Thoreau's thought from that of Emerson, acquitting him of the charge of being a mere imitator of the older man. More astutely than anyone else, Salt recognized the central plank of Thoreau's philosophy of life:

that each individual mind, instead of being crushed
and warped in the struggle of life, may have space to
develop its own distinctive qualities and follow the
bent of its own natural temperament.

Salt stressed the importance of "Civil Disobedience," identifying its radical insistence that society is "to be reformed . . . by individual effort." And he concluded by claiming that Thoreau had made "the most vigorous protest ever raised against that artificiality in life and literature which constitutes one of the chief dangers of our complex civilisation."

Salt edited Thoreau's *Anti-Slavery and Reform Papers*, and he also edited *Selections from Thoreau*, published in 1895. His intention was to bring Thoreau to as wide an English audience as possible. In 1896 he revised his *Life of Henry David Thoreau*, which was published in a cheap edition. Salt went on to become a noted campaigner on behalf of the humane treatment of animals, vegetarianism, prison reform, and world peace, and he also wrote a number of books of nature study. All of his writings show a strong infusion of Thoreauvian characteristics.

Salt's biography did not sell in huge numbers when first published, but it was the most important source of information on Thoreau's life and thought for more than 70 years. For many Thoreauvians it is still the best general assessment of Thoreau's central ideas, and it remains in print. Even if it had been consigned to the shelves of history and forgotten, however, its significance for the present-day estimation of Thoreau would have been assured by the fact of its having been read, in 1907, by an Indian lawyer working in South Africa, Mohandas K. Gandhi.

The young Gandhi in London in 1890, every inch the English gentleman.

Thoreau and Gandhi

Anyone meeting Gandhi before about 1900 would have thought it extremely unlikely that he would become a renowned public figure, the moral and spiritual leader of a nation, a man who could stand up to the might of the British Empire. Gandhi was born in 1869 in the Indian state of Gujarat, one of six children of a local government official. He showed no particular promise as a young man, either as a scholar or a leader, but on the death of his father when Gandhi was sixteen he was chosen by his extended family as the child most suited to gaining a professional qualification that would allow him to support his brothers and sisters. Accordingly, he was sent to England in 1888 to study law.

Gandhi's appearance on arriving in London was as far as can be imagined from the loincloth-clad figure that most people are familiar with. His dress was almost a parody of English gentlemanliness, with silk hat and spats and patent leather boots—even a silver-mounted cane. He took lessons in French, dancing, violin, and elocution, and although these did not last long, his punctiliousness about clothes remained for some years after he had left England. Gandhi's efforts in the matter of dress and his other forays into Westernization were probably symptoms of his lack of confidence in his own culture as a young man in an alien country. His English was not fluent, he did not have very much money, and he was also cripplingly shy. Another problem was his vegetarianism, which was uncommon in England at that time, and the food he was offered by his landlady was frequently bland and inedible. Eventually, he found a vegetarian restaurant, and not only enjoyed his first proper meal but also discovered Henry Salt's *Plea for Vegetarianism*, which linked diet with morality and religion. This book stimulated a concern in Gandhi about the relationship between diet, health, and religion that was to last a lifetime. As we will see, it was not the last time that Salt's work would be influential on him.

The main purpose of Gandhi's time in England was the study of law, and in this he was successful, qualifying in 1891. However, his return to India was not the triumph that he might have hoped for, because he knew little of Indian law and had no experience in practice. He barely scraped a living—until in 1893 he was asked to go to South Africa to act on behalf of an Indian firm that had business there. This routine job seemed a far cry from the high hopes of the London-trained barrister, but in fact the experience was to transform Gandhi from a failed lawyer into one of the most charismatic figures of the twentieth century. And it was in South Africa that Gandhi first became aware of Henry Thoreau.

South Africa

If Gandhi's arrival in England had been unsettling, it was as nothing to the shock of his first experiences of South Africa. A week after he arrived, Gandhi was traveling by train from Durban to Pretoria when a white passenger objected to sharing a compartment with him on the grounds of his color. Gandhi had a first-class ticket and refused to move, whereupon he was physically ejected from the train by a police constable. This was the first of Gandhi's many experiences of the humiliating and degrading treatment that Indians in South Africa suffered and meekly acquiesced in. Gandhi was accustomed to being treated as an equal with other subjects of the British Empire, and he had mixed freely in English society without any hint of racial discrimination. In South Africa, Indians were not only subjected to social humiliations but also were the victims of hostile legislation that deprived them of voting rights, taxed them unfairly, and prevented them from moving freely around the country.

Gandhi became involved in campaigns to oppose these discriminatory laws, fighting in the courts and appealing in the press and through petitions to the British authorities in London. The timid barrister gradually transformed himself into a skilled lawyer and political spokesman, who used a range of different methods to draw attention to and agitate against the inequalities of South Africa. Gandhi started and financed a newspaper, *Indian Opinion*, aimed at South Africa's Indian population, to raise awareness of their intolerable situation and to encourage

Gandhi in Johannesburg in 1900. His early experiences of discrimination in South Africa radicalized him and produced a determination to fight on behalf of his fellow Indians.

As a successful lawyer, Gandhi had the income and the social standing to offer leadership to the Indian population in South Africa in organizing against the repressive policies of the South African authorities.

opposition. He was instrumental in founding in 1894 the Natal Indian Congress, a political association directed toward addressing the grievances of Indians. He traveled to London to make personal representations to senior government officials. All these methods would recur in his later political activity after his return to India in 1914. However, Gandhi's best-known and in some ways most effective technique is what links him most closely to Thoreau: *satyagraha*, or civil resistance.

Satyagraha

Gandhi read "Civil Disobedience" sometime around 1906–1907, although opinions differ over exactly when. A letter from Gandhi to Henry Salt put the date at 1907, and suggested that the essay had been sent to Gandhi by a friend. Certainly, it made a strong impression on him:

> The essay seemed to be so convincing and truthful that I felt the need of knowing more of Thoreau, and I came across your Life of him, his "Walden," and other shorter essays, all of which I read with great pleasure and equal profit.

During this period Gandhi was involved in organizing the first of his campaigns of civil disobedience in protest against the Asiatic Registration Ordinance of 1906. This had been introduced by the Transvaal government and required every Indian immigrant to register with the governor and be fingerprinted. Gandhi convened a mass meeting of Indians in Natal to protest this demeaning and discriminatory law, and those present pledged to disobey the registration requirement and accept the consequences. Gandhi himself was imprisoned for two months in 1908 for encouraging Indians not to register—the first of numerous imprisonments that punctuated his political life. It was during this incarceration that he read, among many other things, Salt's *Life of Henry David Thoreau*.

The precise relationship between Thoreau's essay and Gandhi's ideas is difficult to establish. The idea of civil resistance to injustice did not derive from Thoreau: Such action had a long history in Indian culture. For instance, a practice called *dharna* was used by creditors to recover debts. The creditor would sit fasting outside the door of the debtor, perhaps for several days, until the debtor was shamed into making payment. There are medieval records of *dharna* being used against unjust rulers by groups of subjects fasting en masse. Nearer to Gandhi's own time there were certainly mass protests against the imposition of income tax in 1860, involving the ceremonial destruction of income tax forms. A tradition of more or less nonviolent public protest might thus be described as part of Indian culture.

What Gandhi found in Thoreau, and other Western writers, helped him to focus these traditional methods of civil disobedience into a clear doctrine, which he called *satyagraha*, meaning "truth force." Gandhi detested the idea of "passive" resistance, which suggested to him weakness on the part of the protestors, and he would have found ample support in Thoreau's essay for the idea of the power of the individual in the face of an oppressive state. For Gandhi, *satyagraha* was a positive action—the action of a courageous, loving spirit pitted against wrong. It was based on a belief in "the conquest of the adversary by suffering in one's own person," and accepting imprisonment was an important aspect of this. At the beginning of the Transvaal process he wrote:

> *We believe that if the Indians in the Transvaal firmly stick to this resolution, they will at once be free of their shackles. The gaol will then be like a palace to them. Instead of being a disgrace, going to gaol will enhance their prestige.*

Gandhi's exposition of *satyagraha* encouraged self-confidence in the Indian population and invited them to cast off the role of the meek underlings. Imprisonment was a proof of their firm attachment to the truth. We are irresistibly reminded of Thoreau:

> *The proper place to-day, the only place which Massachusetts has provided for her freer and less desponding spirits, is in her prisons, to be put out and locked out of the State by her own act, as they have already put themselves out by their principles. It is there that the fugitive slave, and the Mexican prisoner on parole, and the Indian come to plead the wrongs of his race, should find them; on that separate, but more free and honorable ground, where the State places those who are not* with *her,*

but against *her—the only house in a slave State in which a free man can abide with honor.*

Satyagraha began as a pragmatic response to a situation and was transformed by Gandhi into a conscious ideal. Thoreau and other Western writers, such as Tolstoy and Ruskin, were instrumental in this transformation: Gandhi credited Thoreau with providing "scientific confirmation" of his activities in South Africa, and he reproduced extracts from "Civil Disobedience" in his newspaper *Indian Opinion* in 1907. Thoreau is frequently quoted in Gandhi's writings, and as late as 1931, Roger Baldwin—one of the founders of the American Civil Liberties Union—reported that Gandhi had a copy of Thoreau's essay with him when they traveled together to a conference in France:

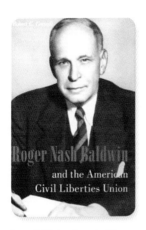

Roger Baldwin, who met with Gandhi, testified to his enduring respect for Thoreau's principles and writings.

> *[Gandhi] observed . . . that Thoreau first formulated for him the tactics of civil disobedience, whose very name he borrowed, and gave it moral justification.*

There is one other important link between these two thinkers. Thoreau was devoted to the writings of Eastern mysticism, and had probably read as much Vedic literature as Gandhi had himself; he read the *Dharma Sastra* in 1841, when he was 24, and the *Bhagavad Gita* in 1845 in his cabin at Walden Pond. He wrote in his *Journal*:

> *The New Testament is remarkable for its pure morality, the best of the Vedic Scripture, for its pure intellectuality. The reader is nowhere raised into and sustained in a bigger, purer, or rarer region of thought than in the* Bhagavad Gita.

In 1855 his English friend Thomas Cholmondeley sent Thoreau 44 volumes of Oriental works, which meant that he owned one of the largest selections of such writings in America at the time. Perhaps it is not surprising then that Gandhi should have been drawn to a fellow "seeker after truth."

Contrasting Philosophies

Thoreau was enthralled by the works of the Indian mystical tradition. In *Walden* he wrote, "In the morning I bathe my intellect in the stupendous and cosmogonal philosophy of the *Bhagavad Gita* . . . in comparison with which our modern literature seems puny and trivial."

In admitting to Thoreau's undoubted influence on Gandhi, it is important also to recognize some fundamental distinctions. One is the centrality to Gandhi's philosophy of nonviolence, *ahimsa*. A significant influence on Gandhi's thinking in this regard was the Jain culture that he had been brought up with in Gujarat. Jainism was emphatic in following the general Hindu principle of nonviolence and respect for life—even treading on an ant was thought to be as threatening to the soul as a conscious act of violence. Although Gandhi rejected much of his religious background as a boy, his later reading of devotional literature in prison, including the Koran, the *Bhagavad Gita*, and the Sermon on the Mount, recalled the religious ideas that had surrounded him in childhood. Indeed, Gandhi's concept of *ahimsa* went beyond the traditional Hindu idea of avoiding harm to others and became a positive activity, inviting punishment as a way of resisting evil. Nonviolence was an absolute requirement of *satyagraha* because violent action would vitiate the ethical purity of the protest.

As we have seen, Thoreau did not discount the use of violence in resisting unjust government, nor did he agree that the state had a right to put him in jail. He similarly took issue with the state for executing John Brown, which it was entitled to do in law. Thoreau's philosophy challenges the right of the state to exercise power over individuals. For Gandhi, by contrast, suffering the punishment of the state was an essential part of *satyagraha* because it was the means of demonstrating the ethical superiority of the sufferer's case. The rule of law had to be acknowledged even while the injustice of a specific law was highlighted, or anarchy would ensue. It is significant that his introduction to the extracts from "Civil Disobedience" in *Indian Opinion* stresses Thoreau's own suffering:

Accepting the punishment of the law was an essential part of Gandhi's doctrine of *satyagraha*, as expressing the purity of the protestor's case. In this his philosophy differs from Thoreau's robust rejection of the state's authority.

> [Henry] David Thoreau was a great writer, philosopher, poet and withal a most practical man, that is, he taught nothing he was not prepared to practise in himself . . . . He went to gaol for the sake of his principles and suffering humanity. His essay, therefore, has been sanctified by suffering.

Gandhi's philosophy is based on shaming the authorities through humility and self-sacrifice, which he saw as ennobling: "The self-sacrifice of one innocent man is a million times more potent than the sacrifice of a million men who die in the act of killing others."

Thoreau in America

While Thoreau was taken seriously by elements in English Socialism and was playing a significant part in the birth of the Indian nation, he remained more or less invisible in his native country. From around the mid-1920s, however, his work began to be taken up by academic critics and the wider public, and to be read as something more than the nature-loving effusions of an eccentric hermit. American literature had not been considered a proper subject for academic study before this time, but as American writers began to receive scholarly attention, so their works, including those of Thoreau, started to appear on school and college curriculums. Thoreau the naturalist may still have been the main focus of attention, but Thoreau the political thinker did finally emerge.

It would be true to say that those who considered Thoreau's social and political writings did not evince much enthusiasm for what they found there. The decade was in many ways inimical to what Thoreau had to offer. In the words of President Calvin Coolidge, the business of America was business, and there was little room for self-questioning, much less dissent. The order of the day was good citizenship, taking one's allotted place in the social sphere, being alert to the Red Menace, and placing one's trust in the flag, the Republican party, sobriety, and orthodoxy. Those critics who recognized Thoreau's reformist leanings therefore did so with some ambivalence. As one writer noted in 1920, "one fears that he seldom knew the sober and durable pleasure that comes of pulling one's weight in the world's united effort."

The America of President Calvin Coolidge was pleased with itself and its success, and had little need of Thoreau's kind of reformist zeal. The Depression of the 1930s would puncture this complacency.

President Roosevelt's inaugural address on March 4, 1933, called for a restoration of American values that were not based solely on economic exchange, and Thoreau's stock as a social thinker rose in tandem with this new consciousness.

This conservative complacency was abruptly shattered by the economic collapse of 1929. Suddenly there was a whole lot less business to go around, and President Roosevelt's inaugural address in 1933 declared that "happiness lies not in the mere possession of money." In these circumstances, Thoreau's demonstration in *Walden* that it was possible to live without material goods became extremely important to the vast numbers of Americans who had lost their jobs and their farms. Thoreau's political and social writings were thus of much more interest to social commentators and journalists, and in a pattern that we will see repeated to the present day, he was claimed as an ally by various opposed factions.

Roosevelt's New Deal in the 1930s heralded a return to liberal values after the conservative decades that had gone before. The general shift to the political left saw Thoreau being embraced in some quarters as a kind of Jeffersonian liberal and a prophet of the destructiveness of corporate materialism, evidence of which could be seen all around. However, he was also taken up by those who did not see a collective solution as the proper response to America's problems. The libertarian right, which objected to government interference in the affairs of individuals and saw self-help as the only way to salvation, found a ready source of support in Thoreau, and he was frequently cited by those who had a horror of the social *dirigisme* of the Marxists. Conversely, many Marxists recoiled from Thoreau's antisocial philosophy and viewed him as a proto-Fascist.

Although Thoreau was firmly on the political map by the end of the 1930s, there was little clear analysis of his ideas in any of the claims made by those who co-opted him to their cause. More often than not, champions of Thoreau took from him whatever suited their own purposes, and overlooked anything that did not fit. A good example of this is Henry Seidel Canby, who wrote, among many other works on Thoreau, a biography published in 1939. Canby's writings emphasize Thoreau's nonconformity and his reluctance to take part in any kind of collective action, and he holds him up as an example of individual self-reliance against the impersonal totality of the industrial machine, or the party organization. He argues that "we must breed Thoreaus somewhere" as an antidote to the destruction of individual freedom that the machine age produces, but he slithers over the detail of how a society of antisocial nonconformists would actually function.

Generally, Thoreau had a quiet war. Where the 1930s had been a period of turmoil and self-doubt, after 1940 there was no room for questioning voices as the American people stood together to face the enemy. One significant Thoreau-related event did, however, occur during the war years. In 1941 the Thoreau Society was founded to generate a wider interest in his life and work—a task that it continues to this day. The Thoreauvians were not immune to the general tendency to adapt Thoreau to suit their own ideas and values, as the founder of the Society, Walter Harding, admitted: "We admit that we are hero-worshipers, but we hope that we retain at least an iota of objectivity about our hero." Harding and the Thoreauvians were instrumental in promoting a somewhat sanitized view of Thoreau through the 1940s and into the 1950s.

Postwar America saw Thoreau's politics relegated to a back seat, as they had been in the 1920s. Although the symbolic and mythic qualities of Thoreau's writing began to be explored and admired by critics, his reformist views were once more out of step with the prevailing culture. In the atmosphere of tension generated by the Cold War, the threat of Communism, and the shadow of the atomic bomb, American society drew its wagons into a circle and dared anyone from outside or inside to criticize. There was a revival of religious belief and of conservative values in which optimism and patriotic loyalty were paramount, such that the intimidatory harassment of the House Un-American Activities Committee was able to flourish. Indeed, Thoreau was himself a victim of Joseph McCarthy's witchhunt. In 1953, the United States Information Service placed a textbook of American literature in all its libraries around the world. McCarthy succeeded in having the book removed from the shelves on the grounds that it included Thoreau's "Civil Disobedience." An article by E.B. White in the *New Yorker* ridiculed McCarthy's campaign by imagining the Senator visiting Thoreau in his hut by Walden Pond and pronouncing him un-American on the grounds of his independence and self-reliance, qualities valued by most Americans. Many writers and commentators

The House Un-American Activities Committee epitomized the repressive, paranoiac tendencies of American postwar society. Dissent from mainstream conservative opinion was viewed as little short of treason.

The long-running war in Vietnam drained America's self-confidence, and was the focus of the struggle between the values of Cold War America and the reformist voices of the 1960s.

found "Civil Disobedience" a useful support in arguing that dissenters were not necessarily Communist subversives.

For most of America, on the other hand, it was back to business as usual, and the general prosperity encouraged a complacent inattention to the serious fault lines in American society. Thoreau's individualism either was used as a stick with which to beat the totalitarian Marxists or was condemned as being a self-indulgent subversion of society's institutions. Even the Thoreauvians, who praised the redemptive spirit of *Walden* as an antidote to the "falsehood and fear and Fascism" of 1950s America, stopped short of suggesting that Thoreau might offer any kind of political solution. That would have to wait for the new decade.

Thoreau in the 1960s

By the end of the 1950s, it had become impossible to keep the lid on America's problems with appeals to patriotic loyalty backed up by state coercion. Public awareness, especially among young people, of institutional racism, poverty, environmental destruction, and unthinking materialism burst out in a wave of dissent, political activism, and civil disobedience on a wide scale. The ongoing horror of the war in Vietnam with its attendant political hypocrisy, dishonesty, and imperialism supplied a constant background noise of social instability. Feeling angered and betrayed by their leaders, many Americans looked for prophetic voices to declare how society should be reformed. Thoreau's time had arrived at last.

Martin Luther King delivering his famous "I have a dream" speech from the steps of the Lincoln Memorial. King reread "Civil Disobedience" several times, and saw Thoreau as a forerunner in the struggle that black America was engaged in.

The most significant figure for the establishment of Thoreau's reputation during this period was undoubtedly Martin Luther King. King had studied "Civil Disobedience" in college and was immediately impressed by it, although more as an intellectual defense of lawbreaking than as an inspiration. It was only after the launch of the civil rights movement with the Montgomery bus boycott in 1956 that King recognized the relationship between what black Americans were doing and what Thoreau had written:

> I became convinced that what we were preparing to do in Montgomery was related to what Thoreau had expressed. We were simply saying to the white community, "We can no longer lend our cooperation to an evil system."

The yearlong boycott of the Montgomery bus service not only brought King to national prominence but also increased exponentially the public's awareness of Thoreau as a political thinker. King's speeches and writings frequently alluded to "Civil Disobedience," so Thoreau became bound up with the black civil rights movement and hence with the culture of political protest that characterized the 1960s. King placed Thoreau in the forefront of this struggle:

> [N]oncooperation with evil is as much a moral obligation as is cooperation with good. No other person has been more eloquent and passionate in getting this idea across than Henry David Thoreau. As a result of his writings and personal witness, we are the heirs of a legacy of creative protest.

King and Kennedy between them exemplified the hopes of the new America that seemed to be emerging in the 1960s. Neither of them was allowed to live long enough to bring their dreams to fruition.

King's Dream and Thoreau

There are echoes of Thoreau's lecture in the most famous speech that Martin Luther King ever made. The occasion was a huge civil rights march on August 28, 1963, in Washington, D.C., organized by the black union leader A. Philip Randolph. President Kennedy was preparing a civil rights bill that would antagonize white Southerners in his own party who were opposed to racial integration, and he had wanted the march to be called off. "We want success in Congress," said Kennedy, "not just a big show at the Capitol." Randolph refused, and his colleague, King, agreed. Realizing that he could not stop it, Kennedy instead embraced the march, calling it a "peaceful assembly for the redress of grievances."

A quarter million people turned up for the march, and among the marchers were Charlton Heston, Sammy Davis Jr., and Sidney Poitier. Marlon Brando marched carrying a cattle prod to symbolize police brutality. There were only four arrests recorded by the police, all of them white people. King's speech, from the steps of the Lincoln Memorial, closed the proceedings. He had delivered similar speeches many times, but this time he had the eyes and ears of the world on him, and he rose to the occasion. Starting with Lincoln and ending with "a dream rooted in the American dream," he attacked the moral stain of racial segregation. Like Thoreau, he aimed at the consciences of those present, citing the fundamentals of the American citizen's self-understanding, the bases on which the United States had been established.

Thoreau ended the section of his lecture about his night in prison with a vision of freedom restored:

> I was put into jail as I was going to the shoemaker's
> to get a shoe which was mended. When I was let out
> the next morning, I proceeded to finish my errand,
> and, having put on my mended shoe, joined a
> huckleberry party, who were impatient to put
> themselves under my conduct; and in half an hour—
> for the horse was soon tackled—was in the midst
> of a huckleberry field, on one of our highest hills,
> two miles off, and then the State was nowhere to
> be seen.

In a sense this means exactly what it says, that he carried on with his interrupted activities. In another sense, the last few words hold the kernel of what Thoreau was all about: Just two miles away (the distance of Walden Pond from Concord) the state is nowhere to be seen. He invites the listener to join him on the high ground, outside the petty restrictions of the everyday, to contemplate something far more important: "There will never be a really free and enlightened State until the State comes to recognize the individual as a higher and independent power, from which all its own power and authority are derived, and treats him accordingly."

King famously did the same thing. His is a political speech, in that it addresses a contemporary social issue, but it is also a visionary, evangelical speech about what it means to live together as citizens:

I say to you today, my friends, so even though we face the difficulties of today and tomorrow, I still have a dream. It is a dream deeply rooted in the American dream.

I have a dream that one day this nation will rise up and live out the true meaning of its creed: "We hold these truths to be self-evident: that all men are created equal." I have a dream that one day on the red hills of Georgia the sons of former slaves and the sons of former slaveowners will be able to sit down together at a table of brotherhood . . . . I have a dream that my four little children will one day live in a nation where they will not be judged by the color of their skin but by the content of their character.

King knew that Kennedy's civil rights bill would be pointless without a commitment on behalf of American society to making the dream of racial equality a reality. He recognized the need not just for a gradual erosion of discriminatory laws but also for a radical alteration in the mindset of the American people. As with Thoreau and slavery, waiting for the due process of law was not enough: Legal remedies "take too much time, and a man's life will be gone."

Counterculture

In 1960 Thoreau was elected to the New York University Hall of Fame, after a campaign sponsored by the Thoreau Society. He had been proposed before, in 1945, losing narrowly in the final vote and being opposed by a panel member who challenged his eligibility on the grounds of his having written "Civil Disobedience" and hence having threatened the Union. There would be no such problem in 1960 when resistance to the state was becoming a modus vivendi for many people. In the 1960s "Civil Disobedience" was as central to Thoreau's reputation as *Walden*, and an edition from 1968 even reversed the usual order of the works in its title, *An Essay on the Duty of Civil Disobedience and Walden*.

By the end of the decade Thoreau had been claimed as one of their own by antiwar protestors, environmental protestors, pacifists, anarchists, naturists, and hippies. A boat used to picket nuclear submarines at Groton, Connecticut, was named the *Henry David Thoreau*. His face appeared on T-shirts, calendars, and postage stamps, and collections of quotations from his works were published. As Walter Harding commented, "There is hardly an ism of our times that has not attempted to adopt Thoreau." Some of these adoptions would certainly have been objectionable to him: The prospect of a hippy commune would have horrified such a devotee of solitude. However, the Thoreau who had written "Use me . . . if by any means ye may find me serviceable" would presumably have been delighted to have had his offer taken up so widely and enthusiastically.

The antiwar movement was just one of the groups that put Thoreau's principle of resistance to civil government into practice, picketing American nuclear submarine bases.

Paradoxically, this listing of devotees might be seen as diminishing Thoreau. If he can apparently be all things to all people, surely this suggests either that he did not really know what he wanted to say, or that he was not being read properly by those who claimed him for their side. There is some truth in both of these statements. Certainly Thoreau shared with his fellow Transcendentalists a disregard for systems and rigid patterns of thought: "A foolish consistency is the hobgoblin of little minds," remarked Emerson, and like Whitman, Thoreau was content to "contain multitudes." He allowed himself a wide margin of interpretation in his writings and the range of his interests encouraged a diverse readership. It was not so much that Thoreau did not know what he wanted to say as that he had so much to say.

The second statement, however, is demonstrably true. We have already noted numerous instances of readers who used Thoreau for their own purposes by overlooking the parts of his work that did not suit their preconceptions. In the 1960s the chief blind spot related to Thoreau's attitude to violent resistance.

Nonviolence

Thoreau's biographer, Henry Canby, had already produced a pacifist Thoreau in 1939 to support his own view that America should not be drawn into the Second World War; he characterized as a lapse Thoreau's suggestion in "Civil Disobedience" that violence might be necessary in pursuit of justice, and speculated that Thoreau, had he lived, would not

have enlisted to fight for the Union in the Civil War. He went on to suggest that Thoreau would have maintained the same attitude in relation to the war that was brewing in Europe at the time that Canby's book was published. In this Canby ignored, or overlooked, evidence from other essays that Thoreau's acceptance of the need for violent action was not a passing phase. In "A Plea for Captain John Brown," Thoreau says, "I do not wish to kill or be killed, but I can foresee circumstances in which both these things would be by me unavoidable"; and in "Slavery in Massachusetts," in the context of a discussion about dictatorial government, Thoreau states, "I need not say what match I would touch, what system endeavor to blow up . . . ."

An engraving of John Brown's trial in 1859. Brown had been wounded in the attack on Harper's Ferry and was brought into court in a hospital bed. Thoreau's vigorous defense of Brown's militant actions in three separate essays was overlooked by those who claimed the writer as a fellow pacifist.

In the 1960s, Thoreau's pacifism became firmly established in the popular mind. In part, this would have been due to simple ignorance of the essays that followed "Civil Disobedience." "A Plea for Captain John Brown" was rarely reprinted in anthologies of American literature, nor even in anthologies devoted to Thoreau. *The Portable Thoreau*, first published in 1947, revised in 1964, and widely used in colleges, was described by its publisher as representative of Thoreau's works, but it included neither "Slavery in Massachusetts" nor "A Plea for Captain John Brown." It is thus entirely possible that many students who took Thoreau as an inspiration did not know that he had ever come out in favor of violent resistance.

Thoreau's close association with Martin Luther King, who was himself absolutely committed to nonviolent resistance, would have further contributed to this pacifist reputation. In fact, King's modes of protest owed a great deal more to Gandhi's *satyagraha* than to Thoreau's "higher law," and both King and Gandhi were rooted in religious traditions that abhorred violence. Interestingly, Gandhi had himself recognized Thoreau's accommodation to the possible necessity of violence. Nonetheless, it was King's nonviolent Thoreau who prevailed in 1960s America, and the few voices that drew attention to the John Brown essays failed to turn the tide. The protestors and reformers who found in Thoreau a passionate advocate for the causes they were engaged with were, understandably, disinclined to highlight potential problems with his views, even assuming that they were aware of them.

Thoreau's nonviolent persona was further bolstered by his co-option by the antiwar movement. In 1970 a play—*The Night Thoreau Spent in Jail*, written by Jerome Lawrence and Robert E. Lee—drew parallels between Thoreau's opposition to the Mexican War and the contemporary rage against America's involvement in Vietnam. Thoreau was portrayed as a pacifist and idealist who refuses to compromise his principles. The opening of the play preceded by only a few weeks the American

THE NIGHT THOREAU SPENT IN JAIL

A PLAY

JEROME LAWRENCE AND ROBERT E. LEE

A play based on Thoreau's imprisonment was enormously popular on campuses across America and helped to cement a definitive, if incomplete, ideal of Thoreau as the principled artist standing up for what he knew to be right.

invasion of Cambodia and the fatal shooting of four students by the National Guard during subsequent protests at Kent State University. Thoreau's relevance to contemporary issues was thus underlined, and by the end of 1972 the play had been performed more than 2,000 times in theaters across the United States.

As the 1960s drew to a close in a welter of assassinations, student riots, and police violence, culminating in the fatal shooting of students at Kent State University, Thoreau was attacked in some quarters as having contributed to America's descent into anarchy.

Despite his popularity, as the idealism of the early 1960s gave way to riots and assassinations at the end of the decade, Thoreau was called to account in some quarters for his contribution to the social turmoil of the time. Solicitor General of the United States Erwin N. Griswold addressed the disorder that was raging across parts of America, and claimed that civil disobedience as advocated by Thoreau tended inevitably toward violence. In a similar vein, Undersecretary for Political Affairs for the Department of State Eugene V. Rostow attacked Thoreau's ideas, saying that no society could survive if it attempted to accommodate the kind of antisocial individualism that Thoreau espoused. Neither official cited the John Brown essays, presumably because they did not know about them. If they had, Thoreau might not have escaped so lightly. America was becoming weary of and depressed by its apparent self-destruction, as evidenced by Nixon's election in 1968 on a platform of restoring law and order; many Americans wanted normality back, and wanted Thoreau's admirers to put away "Civil Disobedience" and go back to *Walden*.

After the end of the war in Vietnam in 1973, the reformist Thoreau slipped out of sight again. Fittingly, in the same year the Thoreau Society amended its rules expressly to forbid any involvement in political activities, so as to ensure its tax-exempt status.

Thoreau in Our Season

By the time of the American withdrawal from Vietnam in 1973, Thoreau's popular reputation had been established. Academic and critical discussion of his work began to move into pychoanalytic studies focused on his relationship with his mother and his allegedly arrested sexual development. Thoreau was even given a posthumous personality test by a panel of scholars who supplied Thoreau's answers on his behalf. This was an echo, on a more scientific basis, of the kind of responses Thoreau had provoked in his own lifetime, when critics heaped scorn on his personality defects. Poststructuralist thinkers also took note of Thoreau, exploring the indeterminacy of his writing and the subversive gaps and contradictions in his use of language. To some extent his critical reputation declined as academic literary interest moved away from the "dead white males" of the established canon. Nonetheless, for the general public Thoreau had by the 1970s become a byword for American values of self-reliance and independence, and he was securely fixed as a pillar of American culture.

However, as the social upheavals of the 1960s and 1970s gave way to the conservatism of the 1980s, the political Thoreau slipped out of the spotlight. Indeed, as the radicalism of the 1960s moved from being an actual compelling force toward becoming an object of historical analysis—or even an embarrassing aberration—people did put away "Civil Disobedience" and returned to *Walden*. The burgeoning environmental and ecology movement now had Thoreau as its champion, as did animal rights activists and vegetarians. The Web site of the Walden Woods Project describes the area as the nineteenth-century birthplace of American environmentalism, and the Thoreauvian epigram of choice became "In Wildness is the preservation of the World." Contradictory as ever, Thoreau nonetheless offered a problem to animal rights supporters with his ambivalent feelings on the question of hunting and killing animals.

The one liberal cause that has been unable to find a use for Thoreau is feminism. As gender politics came to the fore under the impetus of the radical 1960s, so Thoreau was found wanting, evidence of misogynist leanings being found in his *Journal*. He has been characterized as profoundly conservative on the question of gender, and for once no opposing voice has emerged to reclaim him. This may be a further reason his politics have ceded place to other aspects of his work, because on this vital social and political issue he seems to have nothing useful to say. The preservation of the natural world and of fragile ecosystems is safer ground for present-day Thoreauvians.

The arrival of Ronald Reagan in the White House signaled a return to conservative values, and the political usefulness of Thoreau seemed to be at an end.

Thoreau's position in the pantheon of all-time great American writers is probably assured, even if the sanitized, apolitical Thoreau is the one most people prefer. Concord, which had begun to acquire a tourist industry on the basis of its literary and artistic associations in the 1880s, was receiving nearly half a million visitors a year by the late 1970s. The pond at Walden was declared a national landmark

in 1965, although it had been an unofficial shrine for a long time before that. Edward Carpenter had placed a stone on the cairn that was supposed to mark the spot where Thoreau's hut had been when he visited in 1884. In the late 1980s an area of Walden woods threatened by development was saved by financial intervention from the musician and environmentalist Don Henley, and the Walden Woods Project was set up to protect the area and promote Thoreau awareness. Thoreau's family home was sold in 2003 for 3.25 million dollars. Membership of the Thoreau Society, the largest of its kind devoted to an American author, stood at over 1,500 in 2003. This most antiestablishment of writers had become a national treasure.

Perhaps not surprisingly, the Internet is the site of Thoreau's remaining political presence. The web site as a medium for spontaneous utterance might have appealed to a certain strand in Transcendentalist thought, the modern equivalent of the Conversation and the Epistle extolled by Bronson Alcott in his journal:

> *The thoughts and desires of men wait not thereby*
> *the tardy and complex agencies of the booksellers'*
> *favor, printers' type, or reader's chances, but are*
> *sped forthwith far and wide, by these nimble*
> *Mercuries.*

Although most of the content of the Internet does not match the Transcendentalist ideal of the "divinity in man," it is not entirely frivolous to suggest that the immediacy of its transmission of personal experience, without the barriers

of publishers or other intermediaries, might have been attractive to the Transcendentalists' rhetorical impulses. Certainly, as a means of allowing people to share their thoughts and their ideas with others the Internet is unsurpassed—the public lecture writ large for a global public.

As Thoreau himself wanted to "brag as lustily as chanticleer in the morning . . . if only to wake my neighbors up," so there are plenty of voices on the Net equally keen to address their neighbors and to enlist Thoreau to their cause. Most of the appearances of "Civil Disobedience" are on sites related to civil liberties or human rights, and the anti-AIDS direct-action group ACT-UP includes Thoreau in its brief history of civil disobedience. As we have seen, however, Thoreau's admirers constitute a broad church, and thus we find "Civil Disobedience" cited with approval by both the Exeter Socialists and the Libertarian Party of Tennessee. Thoreau's provocative and paradoxical style continues to offer food for thought to a range of apparently disparate factions.

Having charted Thoreau's reception through the decades since "The Rights and Duties of the Individual in Relation to Government" was given as a lecture in Concord Lyceum, we now turn to Thoreau's present-day relevance.

Perhaps not surprisingly in light of what we have learned about Thoreau's broad appeal, an Internet search for "Civil Disobedience" throws up some interesting bedfellows.

We have looked at the way Thoreau has risen, from unpromising beginnings, to the position of eminence that he now holds in American culture. He is one of the undisputed greats of American literature, a figure whom everyone considers significant, whether they have read his works or not. So what, if anything, does Thoreau have to say to us today?

In considering this, we might start with a few snapshots of the present-day political landscape. In 2003 thousands of people took to the streets in Britain to protest against the government's support for America in the war against Saddam Hussein's Iraq. The prime minister, Tony Blair, giving evidence to a legal inquiry into allegations that the government had misled the public over Saddam Hussein's military capability, stated that the allegations were an attack not only on the office of prime minister but on the country as a whole—a twenty-first-century variation on Louis XIV's *L'état, c'est moi*, which might have brought a wry smile to Thoreau's lips.

The war against Iraq in 2003 was the occasion for a great deal of public disquiet in Britain over its government's apparent deafness to the views of large numbers of its citizens.

In 2002, the first round of the French presidential election produced two candidates, the discredited incumbent Jacques Chirac of the right-wing Gaullist party, who had been widely criticized over allegations of dishonesty and corruption, and Jean-Marie Le Pen of the extreme right-wing National Front. A proliferation of candidates from the left and right reflected the electorate's disaffection with the main parties, and took

votes away from the Socialist candidate Lionel Jospin. Almost one-third of the electorate did not even bother to register a vote. The voters from the left and center were thus faced with a choice in the final round of voting between, as one commentator put it, a crook and a Fascist, and tens of thousands took to the streets of Paris in protest.

In December 2000, one of the most extended U.S. presidential elections in history was decided by a majority of the Supreme Court in favor of George W. Bush. Bush won by five votes in the electoral college, although the final tally of votes cast in the election gave his opponent Al Gore a majority of more than a half million votes—greater than the majorities that took John F. Kennedy and Richard Nixon to the White House in 1960 and 1968, respectively. American newspapers and political commentators bewailed the fact that the will of the people had to be established in the courts, that the vital Florida count was marred by allegations of

All smiles between President Bush and Al Gore once the result of the 2000 presidential election had been decided, but the nature of the contest was felt in some parts of American society to have brought its democracy into disrepute.

intimidation and cheating, and that undignified catcalling between supporters of the Democratic and Republican candidates had damaged the reputation of the oldest democracy in the world. More dismaying still was the fact that only 51 percent of those eligible to vote did vote. Thoreau's remark about electoral politics being a form of gaming springs to mind.

Italian politics was bedeviled by corruption scandals for much of the 1980s and 1990s, German politicians have come under scrutiny on bribery charges, and the British Conservative Party became a byword for sleaze before its defeat in the elections of 1997. Voter apathy is a concern in many European countries, and a rise in the number of independent candidates standing at elections is held by political analysts to signal a general discontent with mainstream politics. It would seem that modern democracy is facing a crisis of self-belief at the beginning of the twenty-first century. But do the ideas of Thoreau address this crisis as they were held by many to address the crises of the 1960s?

Thoreau the Politician

It would have to be admitted by even the most partisan Thoreauvian that Thoreau would have made a poor politician. For Thoreau this would have been a compliment—he regarded politics as a lowly form of human endeavor, an unfortunate necessity. He thought that American democracy was a good form of government, better than monarchy or

tyranny, but nonetheless only a means to an end. He never joined a political party or reform organization, which is why nineteenth-century Socialists and twentieth-century Marxists had no use for him: The collective endeavor was anathema to Thoreau temperamentally as well as philosophically. In this he was of a piece with the other Transcendentalists, such as Emerson and Alcott, who maintained a degree of almost other-worldly detachment from society in their emphasis on the potentiality of the individual. We might claim on Thoreau's behalf that he was more willing to get his hands dirty than Emerson, in that he played a part in the Underground Railroad, which guided fugitive slaves over the border into Canada, and we know that he helped at least one slave and maybe more to escape. Nonetheless, it would be true to say that Thoreau was not a party man.

He was not an anarchist either. "Civil Disobedience" opens with the ringing claim that "that government is best which governs not at all," but this is immediately qualified by the statement that when people are ready for this kind of government it will be the kind they will have. It is quite clear from the rest of his essay that Thoreau does not believe that people will ever be ready for this kind of government. Thoreau does not want "no government," he wants *better* government, and he wants it sooner rather than later. He seeks no quarrel with the state; he does not regard it as "a man's duty . . . to devote himself to the eradication of any, even the most enormous wrong"; however, he does regard it as a duty not to support wrongdoing through indifference, conformity, or inertia. Thoreau recognizes the limits of civil resistance and the contingent nature of the relationship between the citizen and the state. He recognizes, in effect, that there have to be compromises between the individual and society, but he also insists that the citizen has the right to resist the government if it forfeits its claim to allegiance through immoral actions.

Even if Thoreau had developed a political theory in the way that Jefferson or Locke did, it would be difficult to relate it to our own political climate. Thoreau could not possibly have envisioned the contemporary power, reach, and influence of the state, nor the extent of modern communications and mass media. This would have made whatever he had to say about political institutions of limited value. As we have established, however, Thoreau was not very interested in the mechanism of politics; his main concern was morality, how people should live, and it is in this context that we can see his thought as applicable to the present day.

How to Be a Good Citizen
Clearly the political snapshots presented above do not purport to give a complete overview of modern Western democracy—but they do share one feature that persists in commentary on the popular view of politics (that is to say, the view of ordinary citizens), which is that of alienation. As professional politics has become more organized, centralized, and packaged, so the people it is intended to

serve have become less and less involved. Membership of political parties in the West is in decline; funding is increasingly derived from corporate donors who, not unnaturally, want a return on their investment; and the political message is mediated through television, with its attendant sound-bite culture. Except for the opportunity every four years to cast a vote (and there is evidence that electorates are disinclined even to do that), the people feel, and to some extent are, powerless.

The obvious stage-management of party political events, the opportunism of adversarial politics, and the culture of corporate sponsorship could all be said to have played a part in the apparent alienation of ordinary citizens from the political process.

The reaction to this powerlessness may be passivity and apathy. The citizen reads the newspaper or watches TV, shrugs at what is happening, and turns away. Thoreau excoriates this kind of quietism:

There are thousands who are in opinion *opposed to slavery and to the war, who yet in effect do nothing to put an end to them; who, esteeming themselves children of Washington and Franklin, sit down with their hands in their pockets, and say that they know not what to do, and do nothing; who even postpone*

The demonstrations at the WTO ministerial conference in Seattle in 1999 exemplified the kind of direct action that bypasses the democratic process to bring a political message to the attention of the people.

the question of freedom to the question of free-trade, and quietly read the prices-current along with the latest advices from Mexico, after dinner, and, it may be, fall asleep over them both . . . .

Another response might be to focus on one's own affairs, to look after one's own interests, and to take the view that other people's business is none of one's own business. Thoreau, the well-known reclusive antisocial individualist, has no time for that attitude either:

Practically speaking, the opponents to a reform in Massachusetts are not a hundred thousand politicians at the South, but a hundred thousand merchants and farmers here, who are more interested in commerce and agriculture than they are in humanity, and are not prepared to do justice to the slave and to Mexico, cost what it may.

A third option is direct action of some kind, and this is the one that Thoreau exemplifies. The thrust of his lecture is that people should first think for themselves and then act for themselves. The form of action is less important than the principle. His Northern neighbors could not with integrity express their opposition to slavery and the Mexican War and then do nothing about it except vote:

> What is the price-current of an honest man and patriot to-day? They hesitate, and they regret, and sometimes they petition; but they do nothing in earnest and with effect. They will wait, well disposed, for others to remedy the evil, that they may no longer have it to regret. At most, they give only a cheap vote, and a feeble countenance and Godspeed, to the right, as it goes by them.

This, as far as Thoreau is concerned, is what Jean-Paul Sartre later termed "bad faith"—putting on to an outside system what is properly your own responsibility. Thoreau challenges his readers to "cast your whole vote, not a strip of paper merely, but your whole influence." His concern is primarily moral and ethical rather than political, although he understood well enough that principled action could produce political reform.

A number of objections could be raised to this philosophy. The most obvious is that morality and politics are a dangerous combination. History can show several examples of politicians whose moral convictions encouraged them to legislate so as to dictate other people's lifestyles. Indeed the U.S. Constitution, with its system of checks and balances, was intended to keep morality out of politics so that the virtue or otherwise of the governed or the governors would have no bearing on the stability of the state. Of course, this was undermined from the start by the problem of slavery, because the equation of people and property was an ethical challenge for which the Constitution had no answer. The documents of the Founding Fathers nonetheless make it plain that citizens' rights were not dependent on whether other citizens thought they were good people. Moralists on the whole make poor politicians, because democratic politics requires pragmatism, compromise, and inclusiveness as much as personal conviction. Evil is not a valid political category.

Thoreau was not aiming his address at professional politicians. He was taking it as read that there was a democratic political process, a state, an executive, a legislature, and a judiciary, and that these institutions would continue to operate in much the same manner in the future as they had in the past. Thoreau was addressing the citizens, and encouraging the development of a prophetic, dissenting minority that would speak out in favor of justice:

> It is not so important that many should be as good as you, as that there may be some absolute goodness somewhere, for that will leaven the whole loaf.

How the state and its political institutions were to respond to this "wise minority" was not something that Thoreau addressed. His primary interest was that someone should say "This is right" or "This is wrong."

A second objection to Thoreau's philosophy is that if people disobey the law whenever it goes against their conscience, the rule of law would become inoperable. This was the essence of Eugene Rostow's objection to Thoreau in 1968, when there were many people breaking the law as a matter of conscience.

There are a number of responses to this to be found in Thoreau's essay. As we saw earlier, Thoreau advocates lawbreaking only in serious cases; most of the time he is happy to let the machinery of government grind away. A second safeguard indicated by Thoreau is that if resistance occurs on grounds that are generally considered unreasonable, the state will have no difficulty in dealing with the few resisters. If the grounds for resistance are widely supported, such that many opponents disobey, then a democratic government is obliged to consider the matter under dispute:

If the alternative is to keep all just men in prison, or give up war and slavery, the State will not hesitate which to choose.

In the 1850s as in the 1960s there were issues that deeply divided American society, and a strong sense that the legitimate demands of a substantial minority were not being addressed. In such cases, Thoreau says, widespread civil disobedience is not the path to anarchy but rather to the restoration of justice, a reminder to those that govern that their power derives from the consent of the governed. The dissident voices are the state's collective conscience.

The Constitution and the Bill of Rights are revered documents for most U.S. citizens, but there can be little doubt that their provisions have been interpreted in a variety of ways through America's history to suit prevailing political requirements.

Lessons from the Past

How then does Thoreau's principle of civil resistance relate to the snapshots of modern democracy that we looked at earlier? There are two points that might be made. The first is that Thoreau is trying to rouse his audience to direct involvement in public affairs, the "pursuit of happiness." It is a matter of personal integrity as much as civic duty. One cure for the sense of political powerlessness is to make use of the rights that every citizen enjoys in a democracy and publicize one's views. It is not difficult to contribute to debate at a time when every political representative has an e-mail address, and when there are online newspapers and activist web sites. It is not even necessary to go to jail.

The cynic will protest at the lack of sophistication of this argument, that an individual really is powerless in a modern media-led democracy in the face of business interests and party politics. This leads to the second point, which is that democratic governments must be reminded that they govern by consent.

> There will never be a really free and enlightened State, until the State comes to recognize the individual as a higher and independent power, from which all its own power and authority are derived, and treats him accordingly.

If the people throw up their hands and say that politics has nothing to do with them, or that there's nothing they can do about it, then the understanding of democracy that we found

Left and below: **U.S. Attorney General John Ashcroft was widely criticized for using his executive powers to suspend some of the fundamental rights of American citizens in the name of protecting the United States from the threat of terrorism after 9/11.**

in the Declaration of Independence is null and void. Post 9/11 this is an important principle to hold on to, because the temptation for a state under threat is to batten down the hatches and present a united front. The Patriot Act and the Homeland Security Act were introduced at the beginning of the "war on terror" to protect American freedom, but many U.S. citizens regarded them as an unjustified restriction of

American freedoms going beyond even what was imposed during the World Wars. It was only in the 1960s that civil liberties in America gained full legal and judicial protection, and at times of national crisis they are liable to be curtailed in the name of patriotism. The executive director of the American Civil Liberties Union in Washington was quoted in October 2002 as saying that the United States "is facing the greatest attacks on civil liberties since the McCarthy era." Conversely, the American Council of Trustees and Alumni produced a report called "Defending Civilization: How our universities are failing America and what can be done about it," condemning any kind of campus opposition to President

Thoreau himself may never have gotten very far beyond the woods around Concord, but the force of his rhetoric ensured that what he had to say would inspire readers across the world and across the years.

Bush's antiterrorist policies. In effect, dissent is equated with anti-American treason. During a period when the Western democratic state is felt to be under threat from outside forces, it is paradoxically more important than ever that Thoreau's dissenting minority conscience should be heard, to remind the state's defenders what it is they are supposed to be defending:

A very few, as heroes, martyrs, reformers in the great sense, and men, serve the state with their consciences, and so necessarily resist it for the most part; and they are commonly treated by it as enemies.

The final answer to the cynic who says that the individual is powerless is the example of Thoreau himself. "Civil Disobedience" began as a lecture in the hall of a village in Massachusetts, given by a man who was widely regarded by his contemporaries as a crank who had gone to jail because of his own contrary nature. It has finished up as one of the most widely read and reprinted of American essays, and its author as an archetype of the American values of freedom and justice:

> *[T]he State never intentionally confronts a man's sense, intellectual or moral, but only his body, his senses. It is not armed with superior wit or honesty, but with superior physical strength. I was not born to be forced. I will breathe after my own fashion. Let us see who is the strongest.*

abolitionists the various groups and individuals who were campaigning to end the practice of holding black people as property to work on plantations in the Southern states.

anarchism political doctrine that all government should be abolished and society should be organized on a voluntary, cooperative basis.

liberalism political doctrine favoring individual liberty in tandem with moderate social reform.

libertarianism extreme laissez-faire political doctrine regarding individual liberty as paramount and advocating minimal state intervention in the lives of citizens.

Puritanism English Protestant movement opposed to any kind of unscriptural forms in worship or Church organization, members of which were among the first settlers of what became the United States.

republicanism government of society by all its members, through elected representatives and an elected head of state, rather than by a monarch or dictator; a way of life that allows criticism of the government and in which position is achieved by merit.

Romanticism literary and artistic movement of the late eighteenth and early nineteenth century in England and Germany, based on the primacy of the individual's inspiration rather than the rationalism and order that characterized the Enlightenment.

satyagraha literally "truth force," Gandhi's doctrine of nonviolent civil disobedience as an active, powerful means of achieving reform.

Transcendentalism literary and philosophical movement in mid-nineteenth-century New England, characterized by a belief in the divine spirit in human beings and the desire to become aware of that spirit in everyday life.

utilitarianism political and philosophical doctrine that assesses the rightness of an action according to whether it promotes general happiness, rather than considering its intrinsic ethical quality or the motives of its agent.

www.thoreau.niu.edu

Web site of a project run from Northern Illinois University to edit all of Thoreau's works for publication by Princeton University Press. It has information on Thoreau's manuscripts, journals and correspondence, biographical details, and links to other Thoreau sites.

www.aa.psu.edu/thoreau/default.htm or **www.thoreausociety.org** Web site for the Thoreau Society, whose mission is "to stimulate interest in and foster education about the life, works, and philosophy of Henry David Thoreau and his place in his world and ours, to coordinate research on his life and writings, and to act as a repository for material relevant to Thoreau."

www.walden.org

The Walden Woods project, whose aim is to preserve Walden Woods and promote research and education about Thoreau.

www.vcu.edu/engweb/transcendentalism/

Web site run from Virginia Commonwealth University with works, biographical details, and other information on the Transcendentalist writers.

www.transcendentalists.com

Comprehensive listing of Transcendentalist-related resources on the Net.

Editions of "Civil Disobedience"

There are several editions, usually coupling "Civil Disobedience" with *Walden*. The Norton Critical edition includes some contemporary reviews of Thoreau's work and critical essays, including the essays by Emerson and Lowell.

Biographies

Walter Harding, *The Days of Henry Thoreau* (1965, rev. 1982) is a thorough and sympathetic account of Thoreau's life written by the secretary and founder of the Thoreau Society, a noted authority on Thoreau. Henry Salt's 1896 biography is available in a reprint edition published by the University of Illinois Press, and some people regard it still as the best general expression of Thoreau's philosophy. Other books focus on specific aspects of Thoreau's life, such as Harmon Smith, *My Friend, My Friend: The Story of Thoreau's Relationship with Emerson* (1999).

Collections of Essays

Glick, Wendell (ed.), *The Recognition of Henry David Thoreau* (1969), although an old book, collects a range of responses to Thoreau from the earliest reviews to the 1960s, and includes some essays that were important in shaping Thoreau's twentieth-century reputation.

Hicks, John H. (ed.), *Thoreau in Our Season* (1966), another old book but one that gives a fascinating overview of opinions during the most important decade for Thoreau's reputation.

Myerson, Joel (ed.), *The Cambridge Companion to Henry David Thoreau* (1999) includes essays on all aspects of Thoreau's work by various American academics.

Thoreau's Political Reputation

Meyer, Michael, *Several More Lives to Live: Thoreau's Political Reputation in America* (1977) is a comprehensive account of the way Thoreau's politics were viewed in America during the twentieth century. It is a history of what people have had to say about Thoreau rather than an analysis of what Thoreau's politics actually were, and is the basis for the sections in this book on Thoreau's American reception.

Scharnhorst, Gary, *Henry David Thoreau: A Case Study in Canonization* (1993) considers the process by which Thoreau went from obscurity to become a literary icon over the course of 100 years.

Walker Howe, Daniel, *Henry David Thoreau on the Duty of Civil Disobedience* (1990), a lecture by the Professor of American History at Oxford University that gives a thorough analysis of Thoreau's lecture and its context, and underpins some of the arguments in this book.

Slavery

Rice, Duncan C., *The Rise and Fall of Black Slavery* (1975) is a good account of the history of black slavery in America and the abolitionist movement.

Transcendentalism

Buell, Lawrence, *Literary Transcendentalism: Style and Vision in the American Renaissance* (1974), the classic book on Transcendentalist literature.

The author

Andrew Kirk was educated at Oxford University and has worked in publishing for fifteen years. He is presently a freelance writer and Senior Editor at Liverpool University Press.

The series editor

Neil Turnbull is currently senior lecturer in social theory at Nottingham Trent University, England. He has published a book and a variety of academic articles on the history and contemporary cultural significance of philosophy, technology, and social theory.

Picture credits

The author and publisher are grateful to the following for permission to reproduce illustrations:

Cameron Collection: 8 , 27, 29B.

Edward Carpenter: *My Days and Dreams* 1916: 76T, 77

Corbis: 11, 25, 31 David J. and Janice L. Frent Collection, 62–63 Joseph Sohm/Chromosohm Inc., 74, 94 Wally McNamee, 96 both Flip Schulke, 101, 104 David J. and Janice L. Frent Collection, 105, 106 Henry Diltz, 108 Bo Zaunders, 109 Steve Liss/SYGMA, 113 Joseph Sohm/Chromosohm Inc.,114 David Butow/SABA, 119 both (Ramin Talaie).

Corbis/Bettmann Archive: 19, 20, 64, 93, 95, 99, 103.

Collected Works by Henry David Thoreau 1897: 7, 16, 18, 23, 34, 35, 38, 60, 66, 70.

Library of Congress/Prints and Photographs: 6, 9, 12, 13 both, 14, 17, 22L, 22R, 26, 28L, 28T, 29T, 30 both, 32, 33, 36 both, 61, 68, 69, 90, 91, 116, 118,120.

Vithalbhai Jhaveri (www.Ghandiserve.org), with thanks to Mahatma Gandhi Foundation (www.mahatmagandhi.org): 81, 83, 84

Jon Wynne Tyson's Collection/courtesy of Simon Wild/West Sussex Wildlife Protection: 78, 79.

World's Great Books in Outline 1927: 72, 73.